Messages from Sam

*A Daughter's Insights on Our Lives Here
– And Her Life in Heaven*

BEVERLY HOLLIDAY

Published by Dagmar Miura
Los Angeles
www.dagmarmiura.com

Messages from Sam

Copyright © 2021 Beverly Holliday

All rights reserved. No part of this book may be used or reproduced in any manner whatsoever without prior written permission except in the case of brief quotations embodied in critical articles or reviews. For information, address Dagmar Miura, dagmarmiura@gmail.com, or visit our website at www.dagmarmiura.com.

This book is a memoir. It reflects the author's present recollections of experiences over time. Certain names have been changed to maintain the individuals' anonymity.

Cover design by David Rivero

First published 2021

ISBN: 978-1-951130-63-3

Contents

Introduction 1
The Back and Forth. 4

Part I
Destined Union. 8
Mystery Illness 11
   Angels and Guides 15
Building a Home and Career 18
Sam's Story Begins 23
The Bulge. 25
The Battle. 29
   Evil Spirits and Hell 33
Home Sweet Home. 35
What a Pain! 37
No Comment. 41
   Sam as a Guide 43
A Creative Being 45
   Art in Heaven 48
Falling in Love with Animation. 50
May I Have This Dance? 58
Gotta Sing 60
   Abilities and Passions. 64
Finding the Words 66
Falling with Grace 71
   Exit Points 72
Missed Our Exit 74
Saved by the Belt 76
A Big Deal 82

Two Peas in a Pod. 86
The Stolen Years 91
Meeting Max 94
My Hero 99
Sensitive Subject 102
A Step Forward 104
   Heavenly Shoes. 106
On the Road 108
Unexpected Reunion 112
New Cast of Characters. 114
The Cottage. 117
Imaginary Friends 119
Italian Adventure 121
Good News. 129
Portrait of an Artist 131

Part II
A New Beginning. 136
   Homecoming 143
Misplaced Emotions 146
Bobby Pins 149
Tarnished by Lipstick. 152
Cake and Balloons 155
Pokémon and Trees 159
A Furry World 162
Medium Rare. 169
Max the Skeptic 175
   Spirit Animals 176
New Kids on the Block 179
   More on Animals. 183
Wrong Time to Cry. 185
The Christmas Gift 187
A Hard Day's Knight 190
Final Films 193
European Escape 195
Lullabies 202

All Kinds of Love	205
More on Soulmates	209
Appearance in Heaven	209
More on Romance and Sex	210
Who Is Sam?	211
Sam's Final Message	214
Acknowledgments	216
About the Author	217

Introduction

If someone had told me a decade ago that I could feel relief and joy over losing my daughter, I would have been horrified. And I certainly would not have believed them. But to be honest, that is exactly how I feel today. Adding to this absurd admission is the fact that Samantha—or Sam, as everyone called her—was my only child. I can almost hear you ask, "How can anyone feel anything short of devastation after losing a child?"

When I decided to write this book, my goal was to share my daughter and her life with the world, reflecting on her uniqueness and our relationship. But it wasn't until recently that I learned who my child really was. And just as important, I have discovered who she is now, in heaven.

During the years following Sam's departure, I have become increasingly aware of my spiritual growth. And I've gradually seen a change in our relationship. If I allow myself to remember Sam as my child in this life, I feel a deep loss. This is something I only allow myself to indulge in briefly, for the obvious reason—it just hurts too much. However, I always remind myself of who Sam is now—in all her magnificence—as a complete soul.

I marvel at all the wonderful details about her spirit life that she has chosen to share with me. I feel blessed. I have been given an incredible gift. I didn't really lose my child; I have reconnected with a soulmate. One who loves me more than I can ever imagine, and who wants to guide me through the rest of my time here on earth.

Although I feel joy when I think about my daughter's afterlife, my life still has an emptiness. Certainly, my life would be more complete and fulfilling if she were still here. However, as a parent, I am relieved that Sam is free from pain and struggles. She once told me that she never felt at home here. Now, instead of facing physical health problems, feelings of inadequacy, and the everyday challenge of concealing her sadness, she leads a fantastic new life full of activities, missions, and love.

Just to give you an idea of the experiences that await us: Sam enjoys playing games, exploring, swimming, roller skating, singing, dancing, creating art, making music, studying, reconnecting with friends and family, playing with animals, and having romantic connections. Yes, that's right. Romance exists on the other side. Sam's life is truly heavenly. And what more could a mother want for her child?

A couple of years after Sam left, she urged me to write our story. At first, she suggested I write simply to heal myself. She suggested that I write down everything I remembered since her birth. Then she told me to give some background on my physical struggles. Every now and then she would say I had a story to tell, but then she would remind me that I didn't have to share it if I did not want to. However, by the end of the fifth year following her passing, Sam confirmed that I was meant to write this book. She had waited until I expressed my own desire to share our experiences and conversations. She acknowledged that we all have free will—and therefore, it had been up to me.

As an individual, I had my own hopes and dreams for life. And as a parent, I also had hopes and dreams for Sam. Several of my desires for this life have come true in one way or another. For me, having a child was by far the most important. From the beginning of Sam's life here, I felt immensely grateful and blessed that this dream was fulfilled.

Unfortunately, Sam's challenges, and her short life, made my dreams for her more difficult to realize.

With Sam guiding me, I have a new aspiration, a new dream: for this book to touch other people's lives. For anyone who is grieving the loss of a loved one, or anyone seeking more spiritual awareness and guidance, I hope that Sam's informative and uplifting messages will bring you comfort and, if possible, joy.

The Back and Forth

When I finally decided to sit down and write, a few years ago, it felt like drudgery. I was inspired by the idea of writing about Sam, but facing the unpleasant moments of my life wasn't exactly motivating. I was determined to fulfill Sam's wishes though, and once I started, I felt guided throughout the entire experience.

By now, I'm sure you're questioning *how* I've been communicating with my daughter. I would love to say that I have the gift of being able to converse with the other side. Although I have directly heard Sam a couple of times, it is usually through the facilitation of gifted mediums that I connect with her.

After writing for a few weeks, I asked Sam—with the help of one of these mediums—what she thought of the format of the book. I knew Sam was with me when I was writing because I often talked to her while trying to recall details. She hears everything I say to her. This is a point she made clear soon after her passing.

Sam's answer to my question about the format came during a session with a medium who had no knowledge of my approach to the book. Sam immediately responded that she liked "the back and forth." It delighted me to hear her describe my format in such a simple and accurate way. I was even more thrilled to know she approved. To hear her affirm what I was doing gave me the support and confidence I needed to remain dedicated.

Weeks later, Sam reiterated her approval of "the back and forth." She also stressed the importance of including how her messages have helped me to see things differently.

And so, let me explain the back and forth. The book is divided into short chapters that recount parts of our lives in a somewhat chronological order. And in each chapter, I have shared conversations I've had with Sam since her passing. Her messages offer unexpected insight into the experiences and emotions described in the chapters. They also include interesting details about heaven. (I often refer to heaven as "the other side" or "home.")

Sometimes, Sam talks about her other lives, before the recent one as my daughter. So this book also goes back and forth between the life Sam lived here and her current life on the other side, with tidbits of previous lives mixed in. From these communications, I have gained a tremendous amount of knowledge about who she was when she was here, who she really is, and what her life is like now, in heaven.

Located in footnotes, underneath the messages from Sam, are the initials of the mediums who delivered each communication, along with the date. The names of the individuals in this book have been changed to protect privacy. "Sam" is the exception—it is my daughter's real name. It is with an open heart that I share her messages.

MESSAGES FROM SAM: Early in the writing of this book, I asked Sam for direction. Before I could finish asking my question, the medium interrupted me, saying that Sam kept talking about "the back and forth." The medium confessed to not understanding what this meant. Waiting to hear more, I didn't say anything. Sam then admitted that she liked it and declared, "That's a good format!"[1]

Sam explained that not only can she hear everything I say, but she can also "replay" my actions and words. She

---

1. JD, September 7, 2018

compared it to listening to voice mail but with video. She has reminded me several times that the reason she can immediately hear me is because she is multidimensional and can be in more than one place at a time.[2]

I later asked Sam what souls prefer to call the other side. She quickly responded, "Home."[3]

When Sam first shared one of her past-life experiences, it threw me for a loop. Before that, I wasn't even sure I believed in past lives. But after a few years of communicating with Sam, I now grasp the concept. More than once, I have asked her to explain how souls can experience multiple lives. And recently, she gave her most simplified answer: "It is a new human, with a recycled soul." Sam went on to explain that we have one complete soul in heaven, which she refers to as the "higher self." This soul periodically wants to have new experiences and learn more, so it sends a piece of itself into a new life. Once that fragment returns home, it merges with the entire soul—the higher self.[4]

---

2. GK, January 29, 2016; JD, July 9, 2020
3. JD, May 9, 2019
4. JD, June 15, 2020

Part I

Destined Union

I met David in college, where we dated for more than three years. After graduating from the Fine Arts program in Graphic Design at the University of Georgia, in Athens, I accepted a job working on a year-long design project. Upon its completion, I returned to my hometown of Tallahassee.

The following year was a roller coaster of aspirations and doubt. At home, I spent my energy looking for a job, but my heart wasn't really in it. David had found a job eight hours away from me, and I hoped we would be getting married soon, so the effort seemed pointless. I had expected him to propose at Christmas. He did not.

Perhaps the lack of communication about our future was a sign. As I waited months for a proposal, I considered dating other guys. The fact that I enjoyed other guys showing interest in me might have been another sign.

In late spring, David and I spent a weekend at a hotel on a quiet beach in South Florida. Though I can't remember what town we were in, I'll never forget his words as we walked along the beach and he stopped to hand me a little box wrapped in Christmas paper. "This is for being such a good sport," he said, apologetically. Another sign? Definitely.

Nonetheless, I missed it.

Dazed and confused, I gave David a half-smile. The gift was the size and shape of a ring box. Perhaps this was the engagement ring I had expected to receive a few months earlier. That would explain the holiday wrapping paper. But what did he mean by "a good sport"? Not exactly the words that most girls expect to hear during a proposal.

I was waiting for "I don't want to live without you any longer," "You are the best thing that has ever happened to me and I can't imagine my life without you," or "I love you so much that I want to spend the rest of my life showing you." Did I get anything reflecting David's love and adoration? Did I get anything romantic? Nothing. Nada. Zip. The neon warning sign in my head started to flicker on, but I ignored it.

My mind reeled with conflicting thoughts. Was he not going to propose? Was this some sort of consolation prize? I unwrapped the present quickly, opened the box, pulled out the jewelry case, popped open its top, and before I could see the contents, a small silver piece of jewelry fell into the sand at my feet.

The sign was flashing brightly now. Horrified, I laughed. Was it an engagement ring? If so, how anticlimactic. I had dropped my ring before I ever saw it. I wanted to cry. I bent down and picked up the delicate silver band and admired the tiny, sparkly diamond on top.

So, it *was* an engagement ring. This was it. That one special moment. The rest is vague.

I said yes. And ignored all the signs.

Throughout my marriage, I wondered why I hadn't paid attention to the signs. Was it because I believed love was hard to find? Was it because it felt like the right time to settle down? Or was there a part of me that knew this union needed to happen?

MESSAGES FROM SAM: Three years after Sam's passing, I asked her if she thought I should include the account of her dad's marriage proposal in my writings. She replied, "That still is part of my story." Sam acknowledged the importance of my relationship with her dad.

Her father and I were destined to meet and fall in love in order for Sam to experience the life her soul had planned. Our meeting was completely orchestrated. Sam said, "As humans, this is one of the things you just can't even fathom. How intricate things are." Timing on earth is so important. On the other side, time is almost nonexistent. "But," she says, "timing on earth, sometimes to the millisecond, is how things are planned."[1]

Sam has informed me that her soul has had a connection with her father's soul for a while, on the other side. They've been in other lives together, too. However, she points out, "Regardless of the connection, we were connected in this lifetime." He was to learn from her more than she was to learn from him. Of course, we always teach and learn from each other in our relationships. But it was more important for her to teach him this time.[2]

---

1. JD, December 10, 2019
2. JD, September 21, 2018

Mystery Illness

After David and I married, I moved to Fort Myers, Florida, where David had been living the previous few months. He already had an affordable apartment, so I had no say in our first home as a married couple. David was pleased to have found a budget-friendly place that was a short drive to the beach. I certainly didn't want to insult him, but I had to hold back tears the first time I saw it. Furnished with cheap, plastic-covered furniture, it lacked the comfort and warmth that I yearned for.

I immediately started working at a print shop as a paste-up artist, until I could find a more desirable design job. Although I didn't experience any symptoms of serious health problems while working there, I knew that the ink from the printing press was harmful. My desk sat only a few feet away from the press, and I was highly aware of the unpleasant fumes. I now know that this exposure easily could have had ill effects on various systems in my body that were undetectable at the time.

I endured the print shop job for about a year. Unable to find a design position in the area, I took a job as a bank teller. During that second year of marriage, David and I rented a nice little house, which was conveniently located near both our jobs. I felt happier and more settled there. Working my way up from teller, I was eventually offered a desirable position in management. But, at the exact same time, David landed a position with more income and security in Atlanta.

We moved to Atlanta.

We both commuted downtown by subway from an apartment in the suburbs. I worked as an actuarial assistant in a life insurance company. Of all the jobs I've had, this was one of the least satisfying. I decided during this period that I needed to find a career that suited my longing to serve. Teaching seemed to be the answer.

At the age of twenty-five, I went back to school to get my master's degree in middle-school math. Before I finished, at age twenty-eight, I added art as a secondary concentration for the same degree. By this time, David and I were homeowners. We lived in a small rustic house, about an hour away from the University of Georgia, where I attended graduate school and where David and I had met ten years earlier.

It was during this second round of college that I began noticing strange symptoms that had no obvious cause. I would become lightheaded and experience a sense of losing equilibrium. Over the next couple of years, the frequency of these episodes increased. At times, I was too dizzy to even sit in a chair.

The doctors I saw were unable to determine the origin of my symptoms. At each medical visit, I was politely brushed off. I felt as if the doctors, and possibly my husband, thought I was either a hypochondriac or was allowing stress to severely affect me. Not having evidence of a physical cause for my symptoms, I began to doubt my emotional stability. Other family and friends had accused me of being too sensitive—and now there was proof that they might be right. Could this awful condition really be something I was doing to myself?

During the first year of these dizzy spells, I began to notice triggers. When I was putting the fragranced laundry detergent in the washer, I got lightheaded. And my perfume started to irritate me.

I changed some home and personal products, and things got a little better. However, my immune system was weakening. Whenever I got sick from a virus, it was intense and long-lasting.

It would be years before I learned that I wasn't the only person having weird reactions to everyday products, and that this condition had a name: multiple chemical sensitivities, or MCS. It's also known as environmental illness.

MESSAGES FROM SAM: During a communication with Sam three years after her passing, she brought up one of my common reactions to chemicals—respiratory distress. Struggling to breathe is at the top of my list of current reactions, of which there are many. Sam stressed, "This is a physical problem, not a mental problem."

She said conventional doctors are not going to instinctively look for this. This is something obscure, and only a small percentage of doctors know what it is.

My spirit guides teased me, saying I needed to wear a heavy-duty gas mask (more about guides shortly). For at least a decade, wearing masks was a way of life for me. Up until the COVID-19 pandemic, I always looked out of place in public. Sam also joked that I needed to live in a bubble, making a reference to the Bubble Boy *movie. I thought that was funny because I often refer to myself as the "bubble girl." She admitted that if I had enough money, I could actually get better from this.*[1] *I know this is true. If I had the money to live on a deserted island with warm, clean air and could pay others to bring me organic food, spring water, and all the essentials, I would get better. Someone to fan me would be nice, too.*

According to Sam, I am part of a small percentage of people who are missing some components of the typical human's genetic makeup. There are certain genes in the body's DNA that assist in removing toxins. A decade ago, a

---

1. JD, October 11, 2018

physician ordered a test that confirmed I was missing some of these. And when one of my guides acknowledged that I'm predisposed to having chemical sensitivities, I felt a sense of relief. This validation finally dispelled any thoughts I had about any mental instability causing my unusual reactions.

Sam claims it's part of my journey to go through this life with medical mysteries. She reminded me that fibromyalgia—which I'll discuss later—had been a mystery to everyone when I first had symptoms. And when these strange new reactions occurred, they were another mystery.[2]

Although she divulged that my soul did plan to have health issues that would be considered weird and outside-the-norm—ones that could not be helped through the mainstream medical community—most of these illnesses were not specifically chosen. MCS is one of these. She acknowledged that other people have the same struggles and that our extreme sensitivity to chemicals isn't common enough that doctors know much about the condition.

I asked Sam how long I needed to endure this in order to learn the lessons my soul had planned before I came into this life. My guides and Sam admitted that I will have some chronic issues for the rest of my life.[3] *Not exactly the insight I'd hoped for.*

Sam further explained the difference between challenges in our lives that we can change and those that we have no control over. In each life, we have challenges that we have the potential to move on from. Addiction and anger are examples of these. Cerebral palsy and Down's syndrome, on the other hand, are examples of challenges that are impossible to eliminate during a lifetime. This tidbit of information is how Sam chose to reiterate that my autoimmune-related illnesses will remain with me throughout this lifetime.[4]

---

2. JD, August 12, 2019
3. JD, August 1, 2019
4. JD, November 26, 2019

Angels and Guides

In addition to the vast amount of information Sam has revealed to me, I have learned a great deal from my guides through mediums. Everyone has angels and guides who stand guard, wanting to protect and help us.

Growing up in a home that I would describe as casually religious, I was taught that everyone on earth has a guardian angel. What I didn't know as a child is that it's common for us to have at least two angels and one or more spirit guides at any given time during our life.

Spirit guides are spirits that have experienced life on earth as humans. One guide could be with us from birth to death while others could change out as we go through different phases of our lives.

Angels, on the other hand, are godly creatures that have never lived as humans. There are several types of angels and they have different missions, whether here on earth or in heaven. Guides offer support and direction, but they can also protect us. Angels are mainly here to protect us.[5] Guides often intervene to save us in harmful or fatal situations. Sometimes, they have to call on angels to do the heavy lifting.[6] Some spirits, like my daughter, can carry out playful tasks, but sometimes they enlist angels to help.

Also, angels help us find things. I can think of a handful of times that lost objects have suddenly appeared in places that I had previously checked.

According to Sam, my angels range in number, depending on my circumstances. I always have at least two. And I have four major guides that have been with me for many years—two of them have been with me since early childhood.

My main guide, Cecil, came in with me at birth. And Adom has been with me since about the age of two, which

---

5. JD, November 9, 2018
6. JB, November 9, 2020; JD, November 12, 2020

is when I started having allergic reactions.[7] The other two long-term guides, one female and one male, help me with family relationships.

Other short-term guides pop in as needed. There's even one that comes around only for the anniversary of Sam's death.[8] When I asked Sam if every person has a special guide for the anniversary of a loved one's passing, the answer was a definite "Yes!"

Cecil attempts to guide me through my general life choices and basically oversees my other guides. He describes his main function as a coordinator of all my guides. And he only attempts to guide me in making choices that are aligned with my soul's path; he makes no attempt to keep me from making good or bad decisions if they won't affect my overall plans. He was kind enough to say I haven't made any catastrophic decisions.[9] Although relieved, I found that a little hard to believe.

Cecil has been a human many times and has been in a few lives with me. He said our relationship was usually parent-child, with him being the parent more often. And not surprisingly, he is one of my three major soulmates. (Most of us have more than one soulmate.)[10] So Cecil knows my soul intimately. He said I will know exactly who he is when I return home. He also revealed that he has very nice teeth and that I'll recognize him by his smile.[11]

Adom, who has made it clear his name is not Adam, is in charge of all my major health issues. He has lived many lives specializing in healing, practicing various types of medicine—traditional and non-traditional. Although he has been with me since I was young, he said he began devoting more energy to me at the age of seven, when I

---

7. JD, November 9, 2018
8. JD, August 20, 2019
9. JD, July 9, 2020
10. JD, August 17, 2018
11. JD, July 9, 2020

was hospitalized with pneumonia, which had a permanent impact on my lungs.[12] *Adom delegates to other health guides for my specific needs. He says most of these other guides are like our earthly EMTs. It isn't always the same spirits that come to our aid because they move around and help others in need.*[13]

---

12. JD, November 12, 2020
13. JD, August 20, 2019

Building a Home and Career

After I finished grad school, David's employer transferred him to Daytona Beach, Florida. This was something he had pursued and we both wanted. Perhaps I wanted it more. North Georgia was too landlocked for me. In Florida, it was much easier to get to a beach and open skies. But once we arrived in the Daytona area, it soon became evident that finding and purchasing a suitable and affordable home was going to be a challenge.

We decided to rent a house while we took our time searching for one to buy. The rental we chose had a small fenced backyard—considerably smaller than that of our previous home—and our two German shepherds were very happy there.

The carpet was filthy, so we had it steam-cleaned. Although I cannot recall reacting to the carpet-cleaning chemicals, they must have taken a toll on me. The scent never went away, which meant neither did the chemicals. Also, the carpet was sticky, which says a lot about the amount of residue that remained.

Before our one-year rental contract was up, I took a job at a private learning center as a lead math teacher. This gave me the experience needed to land a position in the public school system at the largest middle school in the nation, in the community of Deltona.

We looked for a home that would provide an easy

commute for both of us. When we were unable to find an affordable home that wasn't old and musty, we chose to build. Wanting plenty of room for the dogs, we purchased a two-acre lot on the south side of DeLand.

If only I had been able to foresee the future, I could have prevented decades of physical suffering. It was while building this home, working in poor conditions at my new job (unbelievable stress and mold exposure), and sleeping in a home with chemicals stuck to the floor that I became ill.

We had found a young and eager contractor. But to stay within our budget we had to paint our own walls. This was definitely a cost-saver, but in hindsight, our past experience of painting a room or two had not qualified us for this huge job. Applying primer and then two coats of paint to all the walls was overly ambitious, especially when we both had demanding jobs.

The biggest challenge of this task was sanding the "knockdown" ceiling finish at the top of every wall. This plaster-like spray was the result of the ceiling subcontractors' overspraying without masking, or covering, the top edges of the walls beforehand. The builder said it was our responsibility, as the painters, to take care of the overspray.

Needless to say, the painting became more than overwhelming. It took us a long time to sand off the plaster, which we inhaled without knowing the harm it could cause. Unfortunately, we lacked the wisdom to take precautions and wear masks. It wasn't until after we were finished with the sanding that I found an empty bag of the ceiling spray mix, on which was printed a warning about the harmful effects of breathing the product.

I'd like to say that once the house was completed I finally had time to relax and enjoy it, but I was underwater in my job. I taught 150 seventh-grade students three different curriculums, one of which included teaching gifted students—who were not all gifted in math—from the worst algebra book I have ever seen. I also had to deal with new teacher evaluations in order to qualify for my permanent teaching certificate. What was the administration thinking?! Sure, I had a master's degree and great references, which were mostly from my professors. But it was insane to give a first-year teacher the load I had.

There were moments, every once in a while, when I felt good about the job I was doing, considering the ridiculous expectations. To see the light go on in a student is a joy that I imagine every teacher yearns for.

But the stress and my weakening immune system got the best of me. By the end of January, I became too weak to continue working. I remember grabbing my desk at the end of each day to keep from falling over. It became more obvious that the job had played a big part in my illness when I recovered significantly after resting at home for a few weeks. Needing income to help pay for our new house, I started tutoring math from home. I also took a job selling jeans at a store in the mall.

The two students I tutored were referred by the parent of a student I had taught at the school. It was extremely rewarding to see these two struggling students soar after I worked with them, especially since I had felt like a failure for leaving my first year of teaching in a school. The mall job was easy work—until I began to react to the chemicals on the clothes. My father, an allergist, prescribed a mild nasal spray that helped me make it through the long hours at work. After a few months of physical discomfort, I sought out a different job.

I soon found part-time work at a junior college, in an office supporting a program for "displaced homemakers." It was a boost to my morale. The program offered a class for divorced mothers who were unemployed or underemployed and having trouble finding sufficient employment to support themselves and their children.

During this time, I became pregnant. David and I

were both overjoyed with this news. Morning sickness, at all times of the day, dominated my first trimester. By the second trimester, I felt much better, which coincided with the opportunity to teach one of the classes offered by the program. It felt fulfilling to teach again, but I was never truly confident about sharing information with older women who had struggled with challenges I had not yet experienced.

Sometime before my third trimester, I left the job at the junior college. I stopped worrying about financial pressures and became more concerned with taking care of myself and my baby. I joined a low-impact exercise class for expecting mothers at the DeLand YMCA, which was perfect for both my physical and emotional well-being. The exercises accommodated the deficiencies and needs of my muscles, which had become an ever-present source of discomfort since my early twenties. Also, I made friends with a couple of lovely young women in the class.

While in DeLand, I reconnected with Melanie, a dear friend from college, and was surprised to discover that she lived in the area. Melanie and I had grown up in different states, and when we returned to our hometowns after college, we soon lost contact. But here's the strange part: she and I had both moved to a location neither of us had previously considered, and we were both pregnant with babies due at about the same time.

Although visiting with Melanie was enjoyable, she was busy with a new marriage and home. David didn't have many opportunities for activities with friends, either. The busy, and sometimes wild, Daytona area left us both wanting a more calm and friendly environment.

In the last trimester of my pregnancy, David and I decided to move to Tallahassee to begin our new family life. We found a modest home only a few minutes away from my mother, in a family-oriented neighborhood with great schools nearby.

MESSAGES FROM SAM: Sam told me that I have a spiritual connection with Melanie.[1] She and I have had two previous lives together. In one life, we had a very close relationship as sisters. In the other one, we were neighbors in South Africa near the ocean. I was a female and Melanie was an older, wiser man. We became close friends who took care of one another.[2]

Melanie and I are meant to periodically connect in this life. Sam implied that our interactions will help move each of us in a direction that benefits our spiritual growth. Our souls had planned to meet up in this lifetime to support and encourage one another. It is common for souls to plan short-term connections. Sam and I have lived many lives where we were not family, and in some, we only crossed paths briefly.[3]

---

1. SH, January 30, 2019; JB, November 9, 2020
2. JB, November 9, 2020
3. SH, January 30, 2019

Sam's Story Begins

It was about nine o'clock at night on October 10, 1990, when David and I returned from our last Lamaze class at the hospital. Our bundle of joy was due to arrive in exactly two weeks. David had worked a long day, and although I wasn't working at that time, we were both extremely exhausted.

My pregnancy had not been an easy one. But I hadn't developed a serious illness, and for that I was grateful. Over the last few days, my uncomfortable weight had been dampening my spirit. And that night, as I undressed, I noticed unusual swelling in my ankles.

I finally made it to bed by eleven and whispered a quick prayer for relief. Now, some twenty-eight years later, I can recall only one sentence of that prayer: "I don't know how much more of this I can take." Immediately following the "Amen," my water broke.

Too worn out to move, I mumbled—to both God and myself—something about this not being the ideal time. It has taken me decades to figure out why labor started exactly at the end of my prayer. I believe God was doing more than just answering my plea. He wanted to show that he was with me. Reminders of his presence, like this one, have held me up time and time again when many of life's challenges seemed unbearable.

Around six the next morning, October 11, Samantha

came into this world. Unfortunately, she chose to come in backward, so a cesarean was required. Other than intense back pain prior to receiving general anesthesia, I felt relief knowing I would avoid the typical suffering of childbirth. When I awoke after my surgery, the intense nausea and pain dampened the joyous event of having a beautiful and healthy baby.

Kat, a childhood friend of mine, had a cesarean the day after I did—yet she was up and walking the next day. I was not. Anywhere between twenty-four and thirty-six hours after this type of surgery, patients are urged to get out of bed and walk. I was delighted to see Kat when she came to visit me in my hospital room, but this emotion was soon followed by confusion and envy. I couldn't believe the severity of the pain when I tried to move or walk. It had been more than a day past the recommended time to start walking when the nurses dragged me out of bed against my will. I later discovered how minor the pain of a cesarean was compared to more invasive surgery.

MESSAGES FROM SAM: Sam confirmed it was predestined that she would be my only child.[1] *I believe that deep down I always knew this. Aside from a year or two at the end of my childbearing years, I never desired to have more than one child.*

---

1. JD, November 18, 2019

The Bulge

As days of recovery and taking care of my baby stretched into weeks, I finally started feeling strong enough to walk for exercise. Before getting pregnant, I had regularly jogged. But at this point, I was thrilled just to be able to walk around the block.

One afternoon, as I finished a short stroll, a neighbor waved and tried to engage in friendly conversation. He called out, "I thought you already had the baby." Horrified, I replied that indeed the special day had come a couple of weeks ago. I felt bad for him. The poor guy apologized profusely. I later heard his wife gave him hell.

The few extra pounds I was carrying could have resembled those of a woman who was four or five months pregnant. And my clothes hung like maternity wear because there was an unusual bulge at the top of my stomach. However, in no way did I look nine months pregnant!

That humiliating experience prompted immediate action. I was in my OB-GYN's office as soon as I could get an appointment. Prior to my neighbor's embarrassing comment, I had been saying for days that I felt as if a sponge had been left inside me during the surgery. My obstetrician hadn't been on call when I went into labor, so one of her partners delivered my baby. This made it easier to share my concern with her. But she lightheartedly brushed off my absurd thought about the sponge. She reminded me that it was common to have as much extra weight as I did post-labor. Though disappointed, I tried to quash my ill feelings about the unusual bulge at the top of my tummy.

Eight months after giving birth, I was still trying to get in shape. But the bulge hadn't budged. I scheduled another appointment with my obstetrician. This time she took me seriously. She ordered a CT scan with contrast, which meant I needed to consume a large chalky drink that contained barium. This chemical milkshake made me sick. I had to take breaks to get it down without throwing up. Before the scan was completed, dye was injected into my veins to yield more detailed results.

By the time the scan was done, I felt extremely sick. I presume this was from both the barium and the dye. I learned something valuable that day, which would be confirmed in future medical tests: If a technician is unfriendly before a test and they remain unkind throughout, you are most likely going to get good news from your doctor. But if the normally unpleasant technician treats you like honey after the test, you might want to prepare yourself for some bad news.

The scan took place on a Friday. I received a phone call from the imaging center soon after returning home. The results had been sent to a urologist, and I was expected in his office around five-thirty that afternoon. David met me there after leaving work.

The urologist was a warmhearted and thoughtful man with an impeccable reputation. Both my parents knew him. However, this brought little comfort that day.

The doctor calmly showed us the images from the scan and explained that I had a large tumor on my left kidney. He was confident that it was malignant. This aggressive growth had basically taken over my kidney. Both the kidney and tumor needed to be removed immediately. He suggested I get my affairs in order over the weekend, as he would be performing surgery first thing Monday morning. He added that I would need to stay in the hospital Sunday evening for a procedure to prepare the kidney and tumor for removal.

MESSAGES FROM SAM: When I asked Sam if the cancer on my kidney had been planned, she said it was not only planned, but I was meant to have that specific type of cancer at that particular phase of my life. She explained that this isn't how things always work. Sometimes, there are things that are supposed to happen but the details are flexible.

Recalling the ceiling material I had inhaled while working on our home in DeLand, I asked Sam if there was anything I had done to initiate the tumor. She explained that before we come into a life, our souls can make plans that will need catalysts in order to develop. However, in my case, there was nothing that I specifically did that caused the cancer. Once I entered this life, it was going to happen—it was set in stone.[1]

Somewhat numb from the realization that I had cancer, I plodded through the weekend trying to keep my fear and anxiety to myself. I focused instead on our family. David videotaped me holding and dancing with Sam, so she would have a keepsake for the future, just in case there were complications and I didn't survive. We also went swimming in my mother's pool, an activity that Sam enjoyed even at the age of eight months. Of course, she wore a flotation vest, so she was basically floating, not swimming.

David and I shared our concerns in bed Saturday night. It was our last night together before I was admitted to the hospital. I remember distinctly the only heartfelt message he offered me—he shared his concern about Sam not having her mother to raise her. This touched me. But it would have been nice to also hear him express his love for me, or his fear of losing me as his wife, his partner. It hurt that he

---
1. JD, October 28, 2020

couldn't say this, but I wasn't totally surprised. Giving love and attention to our child had been easy for us. Since her birth, focusing on each other had not been. I chalked this up to the woes of being a new parent. The alternative was to acknowledge the loss of love between us, which I wasn't ready to do.

MESSAGES FROM SAM: Being an eight-month-old, Sam had no recollection of the time before, or during, my stay in the hospital. However, she has reviewed it from the other side. She said the time I held her and danced while her dad videotaped us was just another light and fun moment in her childhood that was filled with love.[2]

---

2. JD, November 23, 2020

The Battle

The procedure the night before the surgery set the stage for my ten-day hospital stay. Through a vein in my upper thigh, alcohol was delivered to the already-destroyed kidney. I was told this would make both the kidney and tumor shrink and force them to separate from other tissues. But this preliminary procedure made me sick, and I was throwing up throughout the night.

At the crack of dawn, weak and still feeling sick, I was wheeled to an operating room, where my left kidney and the tumor were removed. The operation required cutting through eight layers in my abdomen.

Today, I still have odd sensations where the nerves were severed and left a huge scar. It makes me think of Captain Hook. I can imagine that in a skirmish, he could have carved this long, curvy mark on my stomach with a bold and flamboyant fling of his hook. Having gotten accustomed to the scar from the C-section, it was easier to adjust to this new unattractive scar.

When I think back on the hell I endured from the removal of my kidney and the large tumor that had ravaged it, I cringe. The unrelenting pain continued far past my hospital stay. I almost laugh whenever I see a TV show where a patient is up and moving a couple of days after the removal of a kidney.

In addition to the intense pain, I experienced other

symptoms caused by reactions to medication and lack of sleep. I began losing my eyesight and had muscle spasms that jarred me awake whenever I fell asleep. And after seven days with no real food, my stomach was unable to function. A feeding tube that had been inserted at the end of the surgery was removed on the seventh or eighth day. I recall trying to eat but not being able to tolerate food.

There are disturbing emotional memories, as well. I remember my sister saying to me, in a tone she thought was encouraging, that I would be stronger after getting through this. I wanted to scream at her, "This will NOT make me stronger." I felt as if my body was falling apart—and if I did survive, I would never be as strong as I was before. As the long days of pain turned into long nights of the same, I had a recurring thought: *I would never wish this suffering on anyone, no matter how terrible they are.*

During my hospital stay, my mother helped out with Sam during the days. And in the evenings, after work, David took care of our little angel. The ordeal was wearing on him, and he didn't visit the hospital very often. But on one of his few visits, David brought my purpose for living to see me. I missed Sam immensely. Staying alive to raise her had become my sole motivation to recover.

I think she was as happy to see me as I was to see her. David placed her on my bed next to my leg, but as soon as I reached out to touch her, she leapt onto my stomach. I gasped, trying hard to refrain from expressing my agony, not wanting to confuse or hurt her. Disappointment and sadness overcame me. My physical suffering kept me from embracing Sam and expressing my love. David and Sam left soon after that.

MESSAGES FROM SAM: *I asked Sam if, as a baby, she had any concerns about where I was during my time in the hospital. As her mother, I missed her terribly. But Sam admitted that she didn't really miss me. And then a guide eased my disappointment by explaining that babies are designed not to care who is taking care of their needs, just as long as somebody is. So, at that age, my absence didn't have an effect on her.*[1]

Although I'm not one to seek special treatment, I accepted all the assistance that was offered to me during my recovery. Fortunately for me, both my father and uncle were well-known physicians at this hospital. Also, my grandfather, who was adored by all, was one of the very first doctors in our town.

Out of respect for my family, the director of the hospital gave me a private room that had an adjoining guest room. This additional room meant someone could stay the night. Knowing that I needed round-the-clock medical care, my mother hired a private agency to provide a nurse during the night shift. Although a different nurse was assigned to me each shift, it was comforting to know someone would be there if I called out for help. Until one night.

During another evening of constant pain, an unfamiliar private nurse walked into my room. She took a few steps and stopped suddenly. Her face revealed that she was disturbed. But before I could ask what was upsetting her, she blurted out, "There's spiritual warfare in here!"

Shocked and terrified, I wanted to ask what she had meant. But I also wished I could ignore it. When you're hanging on to life and don't seem to be improving, the last thing you need to hear is that there are spirits fighting in your room.

Before I could say anything, the nurse explained that I was surrounded by spirits, both good and evil, who were battling over me. Apparently, the evil spirits wanted me to suffer. I wondered if that meant taking my life. Being in a vulnerable state made me imagine the worst. The nurse offered to pray for me. Of course, I willingly accepted any

---
1. JD, November 23, 2020

effort to remedy this frightening situation. I was an emotional mess the rest of the night.

By the eighth day, I felt I could no longer fight. I wanted to stay for Sam, but the constant pain was becoming too much to bear. The pain shifted to numbness. I intuitively knew what this meant. I called my mother and told her that I didn't think I could hang on any longer. She said that she would send someone to pray for me.

Shortly after that phone call, a handful of women gathered around my bed and prayed. I remember hearing them ask God to send angels to administer to me. And angels must have done just that. I felt something that I can only describe as soothing ripples of energy surrounding me.

A few hours later, I was eating food. Two days later, I was discharged and heading home.

MESSAGES FROM SAM: Sam explained that the so-called evil spirits in my hospital room did not come to cause me more physical suffering. They saw that I was vulnerable and that they could manipulate my thoughts. Their intent was to encourage negative emotions, such as fear and anger. My guides, who were present also, said that this event could have been a turning point for my personality if they hadn't protected me and put a stop to it.[2]

Very soon after Sam's passing, she felt it was important for me to know that there's no fear in heaven. We learn fear here on earth.[3] *She also acknowledged there is no anger or hate.*[4]

When I think back on the night of the "spiritual warfare" in my hospital room, I don't feel any lingering fear. I no longer worry about what a spirit entity might attempt to do to me. I know that no one will hurt me.

Sam has assured me that I have had protection since

---

2. JD, October 28, 2020
3. GK, November 16, 2015
4. JD, July 23, 2020

birth. *During several communications with Sam, both my spirit guides and angels have acknowledged their presence in my life. They've told me that they not only protect me, but along with my family on the other side, they keep me company.*

My guides also confirmed that angels did indeed intervene to save my life near the end of my recovery. It wasn't my time to leave. The vibrations I felt were part of the healing. Up until my guides shared this information, I had thought they only indicated the presence of the angels.[5] *Since then, I have learned more about these vibrations. Spirit guides and angels can work together to intensify their energy. They connect to one another in a manner they describe as being equivalent to holding hands. Their union causes a blurring of energy that creates a tremendous healing vibration.*[6]

Sam clarified the two main reasons that I needed to remain here. The obvious reason was that it benefited her life's path. If I remained, she would avoid the struggle of going through life without me, the mother who loved and supported her more than anyone else could. However, Sam surprised me with the other important reason: She said that I needed to experience the loss of a child. And if I hadn't lived long enough, then I would have missed out on that horrible but crucial event.[7]

Evil Spirits and Hell

Since the scary hospital episode, I have pondered why any spirit would want to cause fear or harm. When I finally asked Sam and my guides about this, they quickly responded, "Anger." Souls we would perceive as evil have so much residual anger from their life on earth that they want others to

---

5. JD, December 21, 2018
6. JD, November 12, 2020
7. JD, July 9, 2020

suffer like they did.[8] *It is important to note that there are earthbound spirits who do not want to cause harm. Anger isn't their issue. There are other reasons spirits want to stay connected to earth. Some stay, for example, because they have a fear of consequences when they cross over.*[9]

Sam and another guide said that most harmful spirits are deceased people that aren't ready to reunite with their higher selves. When they are ready, they will "go to the light" and return home.[10]

Sam and my guides also cleared up my confusion about where mean and cruel people go when they die. They said all spirits go to the other side. However, those that haven't made much soul growth have a lot of work to do when they get there, in accepting and learning from their lives here.

This brings up the question "Is there a hell?" Sam and my guides have assured me that there is no hell! But they acknowledge that sometimes life here seems to confirm the existence of a hell, because the worst things that you can experience as a human are experienced here on earth.[11]

---

8. JD, July 9, 2020
9. JD, July 23, 2020
10. JD, July 9, 2020
11. JD, March 5, 2020

Home Sweet Home

Once I was home, the worst of the nightmare was over. The pain was not.

I remained horizontal for several days, while David and my mother took care of Sam and occasionally me. Despair hung in the air. David felt "put out." This was all such an inconvenience. I felt bad for him but was hurt by his attitude. I yearned to be taking care of Sam, and I gladly would have faced his responsibilities instead of my constant pain.

It had been several weeks since David spent a Saturday or Sunday on the golf course with his buddies. He wanted his life back. Even though we'd been together for fifteen years, I learned something new about my spouse during this time. Or perhaps I just opened my eyes a little more.

When Sam was about three, one of my friends asked her what her daddy did for work. There was only one thing that she knew about David's life away from home. Without hesitation, and proud that she knew, she announced, "Golf!"

It was a week before I could do anything for myself or help out. Sitting up and feeding Sam in her highchair was my first big accomplishment.

The healing episode in the hospital and my renewed lease on life had given me a new perspective. I had been given the opportunity to see life as a gift. But more important to me, Sam wouldn't go through life without a mother—specifically, without me as her mother. This thought is even more powerful now, knowing what I do about Sam's strained relationship with her father throughout her childhood.

MESSAGES FROM SAM: Sam has shared her father's current situation with me a few times. From these communications, I have inferred that her death and other traumas in his life have been extremely difficult for him. Sam's overall message suggested David now lacked emotional warmth. Sam said, "I'm nothing like him." She added, "I'm like my mother."[1]

---

1. BH, April 27, 2017

What a Pain!

The end of Sam's first year of life was difficult for me. The whole year had been a challenge, even before the discovery of the tumor and the surgery. Struggling to overcome the pain of the surgery while taking on more parental duties was only part of it. I had other physical challenges as well. Dealing with sore and weak muscles was one of the worst.

Even though I was aware I had a muscle disorder in my mid-twenties, I wasn't sure of its name or cause. My mother had been diagnosed with fibromyalgia a couple of years earlier, and I suspected I had the same condition. By the time Sam was born, I was in my early thirties and the symptoms had worsened. My muscles ached from doing the smallest task, and they were getting weaker, which prevented me from accomplishing routine daily chores.

The realization that I probably had fibromyalgia filled me with frustration and grief. I was a gymnast as a child, until the cartilage between two vertebrae deteriorated. X-rays showed the damage, but no apparent cause. I took up dancing after that: ballet, tap, and jazz. In high school, I continued the dance lessons while cheerleading and playing tennis. Throughout my childhood, I also enjoyed playing football. I would beg to play in my neighborhood's pickup games with the boys and was occasionally allowed. I also loved roller skating, ice skating, water skiing, and snow skiing. I never spent enough time on any one sport to become an expert, but participating in lots of different activities fit my personality.

One day when I was in my early twenties, I noticed a sudden lack of strength in my arms and wrists while playing tennis with a girlfriend. I couldn't even hold the racket when I hit the ball. And it was painful. During the next two or three years, this disability continued to progress. I couldn't move or lift items that would be considered not-too-heavy for the average young woman without injuring myself. Exercise classes were dangerous. If I did an exercise too fast, I injured a muscle. Even slow exercises repeated too many times caused inflammation and frozen, overworked muscles.

After college, I started jogging regularly for exercise. Fortunately, I was able to continue doing this for the next two decades. And I could still dance—at a slower pace, but my hips still moved. My favorite form of exercise was dancing to oldies when nobody was around to watch.

Fifteen years after the onset of my muscle symptoms, I finally received the official diagnosis of fibromyalgia.

MESSAGES FROM SAM: Sam said there's a connection between my chemical sensitivities and my fibromyalgia. And that in the future, there will be discoveries that relate these two conditions to the autoimmune system. She and my guides have mentioned several times that most of my health issues are autoimmune related. Also, Sam acknowledged that it will take doctors getting sick with these conditions for them to be widely accepted.[1]

When I asked Sam about the loss of cartilage in my back, a guide spoke up. This was the result of a bad fall from a jungle gym in kindergarten. I had also injured my head. I can remember briefly waking up from being unconscious

---

1. JD, November 26, 2019

as I was being transported to the hospital.[2]

Whenever I have a fibromyalgia flare-up, I can barely use my arms or hands. The muscles are extremely weak, and the inflammation can cause constant pain. On one particular day, when I could barely tolerate the symptoms, I asked Sam what was going on with my muscles. She replied that it was just fibromyalgia. And then she added, "Son of a bitch!" This sounded like Sam, and I couldn't help but find comfort in her playfulness.[3]

When I became a mother, my muscles would ache from the strain of picking up and holding my baby. If I remained in the same position for the duration of a bottle feeding, it was agonizing. I feared Sam could sense this. Special moments with my pumpkin were often overshadowed by discomfort.

Some things got easier when Sam started walking. However, she was heavier, and I still had to lift her in and out of her crib, high chair, and car seat. I loved holding her, though. What mother doesn't love to hold her baby?

The strange thing was that Sam didn't like being held. It was obvious that she felt loved and secure. She just wasn't a child who needed to be held for long periods of time. On the occasion that I felt physically comfortable holding her, I would try to prolong the moment. In response, Sam would stiffen up and straighten her body to tell me it was time to put her down. I often felt robbed.

Throughout most of the stages of Sam's childhood, she preferred not to be held much. Hugs here and there were welcomed, but they never lasted long. However, there was one incredible exception.

When Sam was almost two, she began attending preschool. I have wonderful memories of picking up Sam after school. When she saw me, she would run to me with urgency

---

2. JD, March 26, 2020
3. JD, October 8, 2019

and hug me. This occurred every single day. I quickly learned to be ready—bending down so that she could leap into my arms. At first, I thought traumatic things were happening to her at school. But the teachers assured me that she was happy. Although Sam was a bit shy and often played in solitude, she really did like preschool. Those three years provided me with the greatest hugs of my life. I still hold on to them with immense gratitude.

MESSAGES FROM SAM: When I asked Sam why she didn't want to be hugged as a child, her reply shocked me. She said that she came into this world with subconscious memories from a previous life where she had been burned in a house fire. I gasped when I heard this, which prompted her to say, "It wasn't horrific. I wasn't deformed. I was not burned alive." But the burns were severe enough that they left her with scars and very sensitive skin; she didn't want to be touched. This aversion carried over into this life, until she eventually grew out of it.[4]

Later, I asked Sam if her lack of desire to be held had anything to do with preparing me for losing her. She said it did not and that it had more to do with rejection, which apparently is an underlying theme in my life. And although Sam wasn't actually rejecting me, it provided an opportunity for me to learn another lesson.

When Sam explained this, my mind wandered back to a question I frequently ask her: "Do I really need so many lessons?!"[5]

---

4. JD, October 26, 2018
5. JD, May 4, 2020

No Comment

Sam didn't speak much when she was young. As a matter of fact, she was so slow to speak that I became concerned. In all other areas, she seemed to develop at the rate of a typical child, but it wasn't until after Sam's first birthday that she spoke more than a few words. Before that, I can only remember *Da* for "Daddy" and *ba* for "ball." Other than the heartwarming *Ma-ma*, she was saying only a few more one-syllable words at the age of one.

But around the time that I was getting seriously concerned, she surprised the hell out of me. First, let me say that both David and I read to Sam often. She loved her books. One day, after she and I arrived home from an outing, I asked her about the book she held while I unstrapped her from her car seat. She pointed to a strawberry and tried to say it. I was shocked. I even thought it was my imagination, as she didn't come close to the correct pronunciation. Then she looked at a hippopotamus and tried to say it. My heart rejoiced.

I asked her to say more, but she just looked at me, as if to say, "No. That's it. I tried and it was too difficult." Of course it was. Going from *ball* to *hippopotamus* is quite a leap. Those two wonderfully mispronounced words, said only once, were all she attempted for a while. But I stopped worrying.

By the time Sam was a year and a half, she was saying a

few more words. Apparently, she was soaking up knowledge but just not sharing it. She must have learned the names of her crayons very early, though, as the colors were the next group of words she chose to say. This wasn't surprising—Sam's artistic abilities and interest were already evident.

MESSAGES FROM SAM: Throughout Sam's early childhood, I presumed she preferred to play by herself and not engage in conversation. But when I inquired about her slow speech development as a toddler, she let me in on another secret: she had planned to attempt this life without saying too much. She brought up one of our recent lives together in which she was the mother and I was the child. She confessed that she'd been bossy in that life and that this was one of the things she had come to work on in this life. She said, "I had to watch this." Sam went on to explain that she came into this life with the intention of refraining from saying everything on her mind and telling me what to do.

Sam has been my parent more times than I've been hers. She also divulged that it was part of her plan this time to look out for me, which seems odd, since she was my child. "Even though I wasn't quite able to do that this time, that was my plan."[1] *When I think back on her teenage years, I realize that she somewhat accomplished this. She willingly put effort into protecting me from the fragrances and chemicals of her friends and the rest of the outside world. And after her death, I discovered she had done more than just tell her friends why they couldn't come into our home. She had compassionately shared her concern for my situation with them.*

I later asked Sam to tell me more about the past life in which she considered herself bossy. She explained that it had been a life of survival. There were several children in our family, of which I was the oldest female. An older brother had to go out and work. Being the oldest at home,

---

1. JD, August 17, 2018

I had a lot of responsibilities and missed out on being a child. Sam said she wasn't mean, just demanding, out of the need to survive. However, she now admits "I could have been a little gentler" and that she actually learned a little more from me in this life about being a mother who guided without force.[2]

Sam as a Guide

Almost every medium I have worked with has told me Sam seems a little bossy, as if she's telling me what to do.[3] *From my perspective, she's just offering suggestions and trying to inspire me in a persuasive manner.*[4] *She really wants me to be my own person. She often says things such as, "It's up to you. You have free will."*

We had been communicating for three years when Sam confirmed that she officially had become one of my guides. At first, I thought that was odd, but then I realized it made perfect sense. As another one of my major soulmates, she loves and knows me so well. So why not? She has been trying to guide me ever since she crossed over.[5]

Sam clarified, "That feeling that you don't have any more [to give], and then suddenly you have more energy and strength to do it, believe it or not, that comes from over here." Sam admitted that without the help I received from the other side, I would have given up a long time ago. In my core, I know this to be true. Sam said all humans are getting so much more help from the other side than we realize, and if we open up to receiving their help, we get more.

She expanded on this. "There would be no point to human life if spirits intervened and took away all the pain

---

2. JD, August 17, 2018; JD, April 13, 2020
3. GK, March 2016; JF, September 7, 2016; SH, October 3, 2016; SH, April 11, 2017; JD, August 17, 2018
4. GK, January 2, 2017
5. JD, August 17, 2019

and suffering." Following this important statement, she lovingly acknowledged that losing her, my child, in the physical world has been a lot for me to deal with on top of my physical struggles.

So why would anyone want to come into a life and suffer? Since Sam's death, I've been told the answer to this question many times. Basically, we choose to come here and have experiences that will assist us in our spiritual growth back home. And without the bad stuff, we wouldn't learn very much. As Sam puts it, "We go there to struggle. We can't struggle like that over here."[6] However, spirits that have only come here a couple of times, or have chosen not to come at all, still grow on the other side. It just takes them longer than it does for those who have experienced life here.[7]

---

6. JD, October 1, 2019
7. JD, July 2, 2019

A Creative Being

From a young age, Sam was exceptionally independent and creative. She didn't seem to need my attention as much as I expected, or perhaps hoped, she would. Of course, she needed me to take care of her basic needs and to find entertainment to occupy her attention while I did chores. And when I say entertainment, I mean the children's shows on PBS. Oh, what a godsend they were. *Sesame Street* was one of her favorites. Later, Disney movies would become my saving grace.

MESSAGES FROM SAM: About a year after Sam's passing, she told me I could ask her anything, and then she changed her appearance to look like Big Bird from Sesame Street. *I can only presume she intended this reference to represent her friendly and helpful personality.*[1]

By age two, Sam was spending a lot of time expressing her artistic passion. She

---

1. GK, October 17, 2016

enjoyed drawing, sculpting with Play-Doh, and creating string designs. She would find strings, threads, pieces of yarn, or ribbons and wrap, weave, and tie them around legs of furniture, toys, and sometimes, herself. I was amazed at the intricacy of some of the creations.

One day she got herself severely tangled up. That was the day I laid down the law about playing with this unique art medium. She could play with string just as long as she didn't wrap it around herself or anyone else.

MESSAGES FROM SAM: When I asked Sam about her affinity for playing with string as a young child, her response fascinated me. She showed an image of someone moving thread around wooden bobbins. She explained that this connected to a past life in which she made lace. Reminiscing about her string artwork during our conversation, I laughed and started to admit how odd it all was. Sam interrupted and said, "It was weird!"[2]

Every medium that has communicated with Sam has described her spirit as artistic and creative. And this applies to her appearance as well. She loves to play with different hair colors and styles. She paints her nails fun colors. And she frequently changes her accessories and attire to match her mood or a project she's working on. Her youthfulness has obviously remained with her.

In a couple of Sam's earliest communications, she divulged that she had come here to be an artist and to bring light to a lot of people.[3] And when she was describing her life on the other side, she said, "I'm very content. I'm in a place where I can be creative. I am a very creative being."[4] Later, she playfully said, "I'm over here painting and doing my thing. So, if you need me, just call me."[5]

---

2. JD, January 21, 2020
3. GK, Early 2017
4. GK, October 17, 2016
5. SH, April 11, 2017

Many times, Sam has expressed her passion for creating all forms of art, including writing, music, dance, and drama. She especially enjoys musicals and movies.[6] *Being creative is an important part of who she is. It nourishes her soul.*[7] *She has made it clear that both she and I have artistic gifts that will be with us always, even if our souls choose not to be successful with them during a lifetime.*[8] *She said spirits sometimes bring the passion into a life, but not the talent. And sometimes the talent might be there, but not the focus, because other things need to get done. She said, "It's always there with me, but I don't always get a chance to use it."*[9]

According to Sam, she is more strongly drawn to a variety of artistic expressions than I am. Although I have been attracted to writing, music, and singing in past lives, my major passions are dance and art. Both Sam and I have been dancers more than once.[10] *I found that interesting, since both dance and art have been huge interests in my current life. However, I didn't come here with enough talent to have a career in either. And with dance, I definitely did not have the body.*

Sam offered the reason why I chose not to have the physical body of a dancer and good health in this life. Without the physical limitations, I wouldn't achieve the spiritual growth that I had planned. Instead, I would have been too focused on achievements and developing my gifts.[11]

---

6. KB, August 8, 2018; JD, February 7, 2019
7. GK, October 12, 2017; GK, July 5, 2018
8. SH, January 30, 2019; VD, March 15, 2019; JD, March 29, 2019
9. JD, April 13, 2020
10. JD, September 18, 2019; JD, October 26, 2019
11. JD, February 7, 2019

Art in Heaven

In heaven, Sam said, colors are literally and figuratively out of this world! There are colors on the other side that we just don't have here.[12] "Magnificent," "beautiful," "intense," "iridescent" and "I can't put into words" are some of the ways mediums have described the colors Sam has shown them.[13] Sam said, "The art here is so different than it is there. You wouldn't even believe it. You don't even actually need to do anything. You just think it and it's done." Even though Sam can create by just thinking, she often prefers to work with her hands. She has even taken up knitting—something that she had no interest in here—because it fulfills a need to use her hands. Sam also likes sculpting and building things out of clay. Some of her sculpted creations are so tall, she climbs them while she works on them.[14]

Sam demonstrated how sometimes she uses instruments to sculpt or mold. She showed herself holding a tool that looked like a short wand. Then she moved it in different directions in the air to create the desired shape. She said, "Think of it like a 3D printer." And then she added, "All you have to do is think of a color and the subject changes to that color."

Painting is one of Sam's favorite forms of artistic expression. Once she provided an image of herself painting, in which she was described as having an effortless fluidity and being ballerina-like as she made her brushstrokes.[15] Another time, she showed herself covering me with a multitude of beautiful colors, just to express her love for me.[16]

Although she can paint by thought alone or by using her hands, she sometimes combines the two. Demonstrating

---

12. JD, August 1, 2019
13. GK, October 12, 2017
14. JD, November 9, 2018
15. VD, March 15, 2019
16. GK, July 7, 2017

how she does this, she opened her hands and, palms out, waved them about, making broad strokes, as if moving the paint around.[17]

She playfully admitted, "I like to paint the animals." Sam loves hanging out with animals—all animals. But actually painting on large animals in particular appears to be a fun pastime of hers. She enjoys using intense colors and whimsical patterns. She showed a bright pink giraffe with purple spots. Sometimes, she paints the animals traditional colors. She also paints flat (two-dimensional) pictures of animals, like we do here. Grinning, Sam said she creates in 2D, 3D, and 4D, using all different art mediums.[18]

Recently, during a conversation with me, Sam began coloring with crayons. She showed herself replicating the Mona Lisa by coloring one piece of the picture at a time. She said it would take a hundred pieces of paper to create the whole image. Surprised, I asked, "You actually have paper, Sam?" Of course, the answer was yes. I felt silly. If spirits can conjure up anything they want, why not paper?[19]

This wasn't the first time Sam mentioned crayons. On the third anniversary of her passing, she sent an image of herself handing me a box of crayons and said, "Here. You might want to draw."[20]

Thinking about Sam coloring with crayons makes me smile. Why would she be using crayons when there are so many other materials just a thought away? Then I thought about her youthful spirit and desire for variety, and I remembered something she had told me: "Here, you can try everything. So why would I want to keep doing the same thing over and over again?"[21] *That is so Sam!*

---

17. JD, April 12, 2019
18. JD, March 7, 2019
19. JD, February 18, 2020
20. GK, July 5, 2018
21. JD, November 9, 2019

Falling in Love with Animation

I'm not sure if Sam's soul planned her time here to coincide with the production of what I consider to be the best Disney movies ever, but it sure worked out ideally for her.

Throughout our marriage, David and I enjoyed going to movies at the theater. We looked forward to the time when Sam would be able to sit through an entire movie with us. From research and my own observations, I learned that most children don't have the focus or desire to watch a full-length movie in a theater until about the age of four. I distinctly remember Sam was only two years old when it happened for her. The movie was Disney's animated *Aladdin*. She was riveted to her seat as her eyes danced to the clever images and her soul moved to the music, songs, and story. The three of us laughed and cried with delight throughout the entire film.

MESSAGES FROM SAM: On the day that would have been Sam's twenty-ninth birthday, I asked her if she would like to watch the new Aladdin *movie with me to celebrate. She confessed that she had seen it already and declared, "It is good." And then she offered to watch it again with me. "I can watch stuff a hundred times if I like it."*

She then explained the differences between this new Aladdin *and the original animated version. She also expressed her love of the first one and said something I had been unaware of all these years: that first time seeing the movie in the theater, with her dad and me, she was not only mesmerized, Sam imagined herself inside the story. She could feel herself soaring through the sky on the magic carpet. She also felt a kindred connection to Jasmine's tiger, as if he belonged to her.*[1]

From that moment forward, Disney movies and the characters they brought to life played a big part in our lives. Sam wasn't interested in playing with dolls or Barbies. Instead, she was obsessed with every animal in every Disney movie released during her childhood. Not surprisingly, Sam owned almost every stuffed animal associated with all the Disney movies made in the first ten years of her life. Her all-time favorite was *The Lion King,* which was packed with animal characters.

Fortunately for Sam, Disney's success in the 1990s spurred the opening of a Disney Store in our mall, which made it easy for us to purchase all the characters. For me, the real advantage of the Disney Store was the hours of

---

1. JD, October 11, 2019

enjoyment Sam experienced while playing there. We went often. She would hug the stuffed animals while watching or dancing to the music videos on the large screen at the back of the store. Then, later, a family member or I would return around her birthday, or other special occasion, to purchase a couple of the animals as gifts.

MESSAGES FROM SAM: Just as I did during my phone calls with Sam when she was here, I now often ask her to tell me everything she's been doing in heaven. One day, she answered by showing off her playful personality. She illustrated a place surrounded by fun activities. In it, she moved around like a child let loose in an FAO Schwarz toy store. She threw herself backward into a huge pile of stuffed animals of all sizes. Then she got out and jumped back in. She talked about the place resembling a carnival. "Not the fun house, though." I presume that meant she was like me and did not enjoy the fun house.[2]

Being an only child, Sam loved the idea of having the companionship of a pet. She begged for a dog throughout her childhood. For several reasons, I postponed granting that wish. It only makes sense that Sam clung to her stuffed animals for friendship and love. And boy, did she love them!

Although it will always haunt me that Sam never got her dog, for a short time as an older child she had a hamster, and then in high school, a fish. She also had a cat, named Misty, in college. Misty was a gift from the parents of her high

---

2. JD, August 20, 2019

school boyfriend. Sam cherished this cat. And I have no doubt that Misty took part in welcoming Sam upon her arrival on the other side.

MESSAGES FROM SAM: In many communications, Sam has proclaimed her love for animals. Several times she has appeared with a dog or cat—either in her arms, around her neck, or next to her. At least three times, she has brought Misty with her.[3]

Sam has also been with the deceased pets of other family members who are still living. "I greet everybody's animal." But after making this announcement, she clarified that she meant she greets the animals of people she knew here. Then she revealed her tentative plans for being a veterinarian in a future life.[4]

Her tremendous love of animals has become more

---

3. CL, January 1, 2016; JF, September 7, 2016; SH, November 23, 2016; JD, September 21, 2018; JD, February 7, 2019; MG, November 1, 2019
4. JD, October 29, 2019; CL, January 1, 2019

evident throughout our conversations. And to my delight, she has informed me that my soul also has a strong connection to animals. Sam "hangs out" with all sorts of animals, and she often creates fun experiences with them.[5] During one communication, Sam dressed herself in a tuxedo as a circus ringmaster. Then she showed bears performing to music. She wanted me to know that the animals enjoy playing with her. It is by choice and only for fun.[6]

While I was writing this book, Sam was spending a lot of time with big animals. She mostly mentioned elephants, horses, and giraffes.[7] Sam has brought up giraffes in several instances. The first time, she pictured herself surrounded by a variety of animals, with giraffes leaning down toward her. The next time, one giraffe bent down and she fed him.[8] But hearing she paints on the actual giraffes, as well as other large animals, is what delights me the most.[9]

With their picturesque scenes and colorful creatures, animated shows captivated Sam. Even her artwork involved make-believe characters. At night, she would dream about the characters she had watched on TV or in movies. When she was a teenager, Sam told me those dreams were sometimes animated. It wasn't a surprise to hear that she had vivid dreams with a full range of colors—I did also. I still do. We are both very visual people. But I'd never dreamed in animation or heard of anyone who could. This amazed me.

This fascination with and love of animation was a driving force in Sam's childhood activities, and later, her career goals.

---

5. BH, April 27, 2017; BH, Early 2018; JD, November 9, 2018; JD, January 13, 2020
6. JD, August 15, 2019; JD, August 20, 2019
7. JD, March 7, 2019
8. BH, April 27, 2017; BH, Early 2018
9. JD, March 7, 2019

MESSAGES FROM SAM: *Sam still loves to watch animated movies, but she enjoys other movies as well. Apparently, spirits can watch our movies any time they want. Movies are also created on the other side. However, our movies are inspired by their movies. "Humans would do a lot less without us," she said teasingly. She also said that if she watches a movie and doesn't like the ending, she just changes it.*[10]

One year after her passing, Sam astonished a medium by showing up as a colorful animated crow. Unaware that Sam's life here centered around animation, he was taken with her sophisticated abilities in this art form. I smiled. Coincidence or not, I had recently seen crows in my backyard for the first time ever, just a few days before this session.[11]

Two years after her passing, Sam shared her biggest art endeavor since returning home to heaven. Interestingly, it tied into her love of animation from her life here. She started the conversation by telling me she was designing in heaven. Okay, I thought. No surprise there. But then she began revealing these incredible animated "worlds," as she called them. They resembled beautiful paintings, but they were so much more. Spirits could actually enter them.[12]

Once inside a world, spirits could smell and feel the environment and interact with their surroundings. It made me think of the colorful drawings that Mary, Bert, and the Banks children jumped into in the Disney movie Mary Poppins.

By this point, Sam had already become known for these worlds on the other side. She created different types for others to experience and enjoy. And spirits were asking her to design custom ones. The worlds she shared during our communications included a jungle, a beach, a tropical island,

---

10. JD, September 18, 2019
11. GK, July 6, 2016
12. JD, January 13, 2020

and one just for animals.[13] She said that sometimes she created animals or people to be in them. And once, she made a brightly colored world with made-up people performing a dance-like martial art.

During another conversation, when I asked her to tell me more about her creations, she told me she'd made a small deserted island just for herself. She had also created an underwater world, where she likes to swim. "I can even be under there, because you don't need to be able to breathe."

Just as she had done before, she demonstrated her movements in forming these creations. Waving her hands around with palms opened and out, she said, "I need to move my hands to direct the energy. Between what I'm thinking and the way I move my hands, I can create this world." And then she snapped her fingers and said, "Just like that, and it can be gone or be something totally different."[14]

Sam explained that studying animation when she was here added to her skills and knowledge. And she informed me that she can create her worlds realistically, as well as in animation.[15] Not every soul can create art like she can. On the other side, souls have certain gifts and abilities.[16] "This is kind of a weird way to word it, but we're not all equal over here." Then she said, "We are in love. In love, we're all equal. But in our abilities, our skills, our knowledge, our experiences, we're not all equal." She emphasized, "Every life that we live helps us."[17]

It seemed important to Sam that I accept that spirits, like her, send visions to people down here to inspire them, whether for a book, movie, or something else creative. "Most of the time, if not all the time, that's all channeled information." And she proudly said that images from her worlds

---

13. BH, April 27, 2017
14. JD, January 8, 2019
15. JD, March 26, 2020
16. JD, August 17, 2018
17. JD, April 12, 2019

are being used to inspire humans here.[18]

Animation truly was a lifelong passion for Sam when she was alive. And it appears to be a field of art that has given her new direction since returning home. When a medium asked her what she would want to do if she were still alive, Sam expressed her desire to work on children's animated shows, with the intent of helping children open their minds and hearts. She said helping children on earth is work she is already doing from the other side.[19]

There are so many things I look forward to experiencing after I leave here. And being able to visit Sam's worlds is one of the most exciting. Sam promised she would create one just for me![20]

---

18. JD, September 18, 2019; March 26, 2020
19. GK, July 5, 2018
20. JD, September 18, 2019

May I Have This Dance?

In addition to Disney movies, other terrific children's films came out during Sam's youth. Not caring whether a movie's characters were animated, puppets, Claymation, or real people, Sam loved all the popular children's movies.

It became a cherished ritual for us to see movies at the theater when they first came out. These occasions became the best memories of my life. It wasn't the movies themselves that made them extraordinary. It was how we chose to conclude our time together in the theater.

Fantastic songs always played at the end of the movies. Often, they were renditions of a catchy, upbeat song from the show. While everyone was leaving the theater, we would scurry to the front. When we reached the bare floor in front of the screen, we would grab each other's hands and dance until the music stopped. Certainly, we weren't accomplished dancers. But we twirled, swayed, and twisted to our hearts' content.

I love to dance. And what could be better than doing the thing I love with the sunshine of my life? Dancing with Sam always brought unsurpassed joy.

MESSAGES FROM SAM: At bedtime, when I'm talking to Sam, I often express my desire to dance with her as soon as we are together. Although I can't hear her response, I know she's listening. This constant reminder is my way of saying,

"Please make sure it's on the schedule when I arrive."

Then one day, to my surprise, she brought it up. Sam was acknowledging my sadness about not getting to dance at her wedding. Then she brought me to tears with what she said next. "Don't worry, as soon as you get here, we'll dance." And then she demonstrated the type of dance she and I did at the end of the movies. She went on to say that when it's my time and I cross over, it will be like the end of the movie. And when I reach her, the song will play.[1]

Although I'm no longer able to do much dancing without injuring my muscles, I sometimes cut loose with a few dance moves when I'm walking. I enjoy walking—more like strolling these days—while listening to songs on an old iPod that Sam gave me years ago. On a good day, when I'm feeling strong, I can break out into dance several times during my walk. Although it wouldn't stop me, only occasionally does anyone see me because I walk in an empty parking lot. Since I'm careful not to accentuate my movements, I probably don't look too ridiculous. There are just some songs that unleash that inner freedom in all of us. It's in these moments that I know Sam is dancing with me.

MESSAGES FROM SAM: A year after her passing, Sam showed a beautiful image of herself dancing in light all around me.[2] And then three years after her passing, she stressed how important it was for me to know she was still dancing at my side.[3]

---

1. JD, December 11, 2018
2. GK, October 17, 2016
3. KB, August 8, 2018

Gotta Sing

When I reflect on the unique behaviors Sam displayed as a young child, her fear of singing comes to the forefront.

Just before turning three, Sam started preschool. As part of the weekly curriculum, every class had an hour of music, during which singing was the primary activity. I use the term "singing" loosely. A group of two- and three-year-olds singing can make a sound that's anything but musical.

After a few weeks, one of Sam's teachers informed me that Sam didn't like going to music class. The teachers had to actually carry her there. Upon her arrival in the music room, Sam would lie on the floor, face down, listening to the other children sing until the class was over. This unusual behavior lasted throughout two of her three years in preschool. Sam couldn't verbalize her feelings at this age, so no one knew why. Did she not like singing? Was she afraid she sounded worse than the other squawking children? Or did she just believe she didn't have the ability to sing?

After watching Sam struggle with intimidation in other areas during the first eight years of her life, I believed she had convinced herself that she couldn't do what other children could. But I never knew for sure why Sam was the way she was during those early years.

At some point during her preschool years, Sam started singing the appealing tunes from the Disney movies and other children's shows at home. She loved listening to the songs over and over. And although her singing voice was barely audible, she often sang along. I can still hear the songs from *Sesame Street* and *Barney* playing in my head, an annoying condition common to many parents.

As a teenager, Sam enjoyed singing enough to join the chorus for her last two years of high school. By then, I had concluded that her apparent dislike for singing as a young child had to do with her insecurities.

MESSAGES FROM SAM: Many times since her passing, Sam has expressed her love for singing and music. Both are very important to her soul and have assisted in the development of her creative and free-spirited personality. Although she wasn't that comfortable singing publicly in this life, Sam always enjoyed it. She also acknowledged that music always made her feel better.[1]

When I asked her to share a couple of her best moments in this life, she immediately brought up music, singing, and being in the chorus. She again stressed the importance of music. Being musical has been a predominant talent in many of her other lives.[2]

At first, I was a little surprised by her statement that singing is such an essential part of her soul. I had known Sam enjoyed chorus in high school, but I wasn't aware of her strong connection to expressing herself through song. This might have been because I rarely heard her sing. And to be honest, when I did, she didn't seem gifted in that area. As her mother, I made a point not to discourage her from any interest she had, but I would have been more encouraging had I known about her real yearnings. I felt relief when she made a reference to this life and finally acknowledged, "I wasn't that good of a singer."[3]

---

1. JD, October 5, 2018; JD, March 29, 2019
2. JD, December 11, 2018
3. JD, October 5, 2018

When Sam looks back on her time in the school chorus, she wishes she hadn't been so self-conscious. "I wish I had been more secure with it... and just done it with all my heart. Now, over here, I don't care. You should see me perform now."[4]

Apparently, Sam sings all the time. She said, "I'm always performing." Playfully, she continued. "It's just that sometimes people aren't watching." She said it's rarely just her singing. She described a type of performance where one person starts to sing and then a bunch of others jump in—like a flash mob.[5]

Sam has excelled as a singer and musician in several lifetimes. She clarified, "I've never been a famous singer, though." As a musician, she was considered professional enough to make money. However, she wasn't good enough to be in history books. "Music for me has been more about freedom and opening up. And just the feeling it gives you."[6] *And, she claimed, "There's always music around me."*[7]

In past lives, she has played a little piano and flute, but her favorite instruments are those with strings—like the guitar, violin, fiddle, and banjo. She's also played instruments that no longer exist on earth.[8]

The first time Sam revealed her affinity for playing musical instruments, she flashed an image of the violin.[9] *The second time was a year later, when she revealed that she had been partial to the violin in a particular life.*[10]

Later, Sam admitted she was even better on the fiddle than the violin. I believe she made a distinction between the two instruments because of the customary style of music

---

4. JD, December 11, 2018
5. JD, August 31, 2019
6. JD, October 5, 2018; JD, October 26, 2018
7. JD, December 11, 2018
8. JD, May 4, 2020
9. SH, July 2017
10. JD, October 5, 2018

in those particular lives. She had one life as a male fiddle player and one as a female. She proudly pronounced, "I played a mean fiddle." She received a lot of recognition as the female player. However, in that incarnation, she drank a little too much and led a wild life.[11]

During at least two conversations, Sam has shown herself playing the guitar and ukulele.[12] Once, she provided a close-up image of herself playing the guitar left-handed. Having fun, she said, "Believe it or not, I can be left- or right-handed."[13]

Throughout our years of communication, I have found Sam's messages about music amusing. Always fun-loving, she has been seen and heard listening to or dancing to music. Once, she donned headphones and said "I can hear you" before announcing that the music wouldn't prevent her from hearing our conversation.[14] Another day, when she showed up singing and dancing, the medium admitted to not knowing the song. So Sam informed her it was a Diana Ross song.[15] I found this funny because a few months earlier, Sam had played a medley of several upbeat Motown songs and gave the impression of being in a Motown phase.[16] But to illustrate her diverse tastes, she has played a variety of music during our communications.[17]

I believe the intent of all these musical exhibitions has been to show me more of who Sam really is. She still has the youthful and fun personality of my daughter. And now I've been introduced to the part of her soul that deeply loves music and dance.[18]

Even though Sam divides her energy between many

---
11. JD, May 4, 2020
12. JD, March 29, 2019
13. VD, March 15, 2019
14. JF, September 7, 2016
15. JD, June 15, 2020
16. JD, September 18, 2019
17. JD, July 18, 2018
18. BH, April 27, 2017; BH, Early 2018; JD, May 4, 2020

interests and missions, she's always doing something that involves music. A year or so ago, she informed me that she was writing a song for someone down here. "We can write music over here." She seemed delighted to share this. "A lot of people get their inspiration from us over here." She gave an example of musicians waking up and immediately writing down something that came to them. However, she made the point that we have the free will to use the information or not. "We give people a lot of inspiration that they never do anything with." I have been told several times that Sam inspires humans in other art forms, as well.[19]

Abilities and Passions

If music and singing are so important to her soul, why didn't Sam bring her talent into her more recent life with me? The answer to this has been explained to me several times. Apparently, we choose the abilities and attributes we want to have in a life. And these decisions are based on the lessons we want to learn. There are a multitude of factors that affect our lives, so a lot of planning goes into making sure we don't set ourselves up to fail in achieving our goals.

As spirits who come into lives on earth, we try out different interests. And as the lifetimes go by, we tend to carry with us the things in which we excel. But here's where it gets interesting. As mentioned before, a soul might come into a lifetime where they have a passion for something but decide not to be very good at it. And for various reasons, many souls do this. Even though they've planned to block their ability, the passion is still there from having it for so many lifetimes.[20]

Sam explained further. "Sometimes, we can filter both out." This hit home with me. I asked her if I had blocked both my artistic ability and passion in this life. She

---

19. JD, March 29, 2019
20. JD, March 29, 2019

acknowledged that to some extent I had. She explained that there's something for us to learn in the struggle of having passion without the ability. But in my case, since I also lack some of the passion, it makes creating art feel like work that I need to do. All my life, I've struggled with the desire to create, and I've always found the process tedious, as if it's work that has to be accomplished in order to feel complete. The joy is missing. According to Sam, if I had come in with my soul's true passion for creating art, I would have gone crazy without the talent to match it.

In this life, family and friends might claim that I am an artist but not a great one. I've always felt being an artist didn't come easily and wasn't fun. There was always this guilt that I was wasting a gift God gave me.[21] *I now feel relieved to know that it's important for me not to be a successful artist in this life.*

Because of Sam's growth from having numerous lives, she divulged that she will no longer block her artistic ability. "The artistic gift and the artistic passion will be with me in every lifetime now, even if I come into a life where I decide not to be successful at it." And by success, I believe she meant having a career that could financially support her.[22]

---

21. JD, April 13, 2020
22. JD, March 29, 2019

Finding the Words

After overcoming her fear of singing in music class, Sam graduated from preschool with the confidence of a typical child ready for kindergarten. Or so I thought.

The first couple of days at the big elementary school were exciting and fun. But by the end of the week, Sam started to dread going to school. She seemed upset about something taking place in the classroom. By week two, this dread included an element of fear. After a little prying, I discovered the real problem. Sam and her classmates were expected to write a complete sentence every morning. These sentences were written in a journal, and the teacher would make corrections for the students to review.

I couldn't believe what I was hearing. Although Sam knew the alphabet and the basic sounds of each letter, she certainly didn't know how to correctly spell and compose a sentence. She had just started kindergarten. Who in the world expected these children to be able to correctly write sentences at this stage of learning?

Keeping my cool, I contacted the teacher. She explained that the school had a program that incorporated a phonetic approach to teaching writing. The students were required to write sentences by sounding out the words. Although that sounded like a worthwhile learning exercise, I knew that students needed more than one technique in learning to write and read. Shouldn't they be teaching sight words along with phonetics?

Once I'd emphasized that Sam feared coming to school, the teacher explained that the students weren't expected to write or spell correctly, and that by utilizing her corrections, they would eventually learn. I still wasn't thrilled with the one-sided approach, but at least I understood what was happening.

I suspected it was just like the music classes in preschool. Sam believed she was supposed to already know how to write and that all the others were literary geniuses. I eventually convinced Sam that she wasn't expected to write a perfect sentence. Life slowly got better.

MESSAGES FROM SAM: When I asked Sam about her year in kindergarten, I was once again shocked by her response. That initial struggle of learning to write sentences wasn't her most significant memory of that year. At first, she said, "I hated it." Then she elaborated. She didn't care for the teacher, who looked angry and spoke sharply.

I frowned upon hearing this. I do remember that about the teacher. Sam also said she didn't like the smell of the classroom, which reeked of old dirty crayons. It makes sense—there were always baskets of old crayons in the centers of the tables. With my sensitivities to smell, I was amazed that I didn't remember that.

Sam admitted that her dislike for kindergarten was more about the change. "Really, I was anxious." She said she was prone to sensory overload. Things would become too much and she would need to slip away for a while, but she couldn't do that in kindergarten.

Boy, did this ring a bell. I remembered all the times throughout her childhood that Sam had wandered off because she couldn't handle her insecurities and self-consciousness. Until now, I hadn't known about the sensory overload, though. I feel lousy when I think about. In retrospect, it's all very clear.

When I inquired further, Sam confirmed that composing the sentences caused her frustration. She said it was because she had more of an artistic mind and it felt foreign to her, like she was never going to get it. It confused her, and she didn't like to be confused. Although she fought against the feeling, she clarified that she was actually okay. However, she did say, "It was too structured. I didn't like it. And I couldn't enjoy it—the learning."[1]

Thinking about those first two weeks of kindergarten reminds me of the extreme anguish I felt whenever Sam was upset, sick, or suffering in any way. As a parent, my heart aches when I reflect on Sam's disappointments and hurts.

MESSAGES FROM SAM: It touches me whenever Sam randomly brings up something about our relationship. During a conversation about how safe she felt knowing that I was always watching over her, she brought up my constant concern for her well-being. She acknowledged the anxiety I felt regarding her emotional stress, even when she was a young child in school. She said some part of me was always concerned and worried about how she was doing, how she was feeling, and how she was experiencing things.[2]

By the end of elementary school, Sam had added writing to the list of creative projects that occupied her free time. Even in college,

---

1. JD, November 9, 2018
2. SH, October 2, 2016

when she was overwhelmed with schoolwork, she was always working on a story. When I think back on Sam's unfortunate introduction to writing, I only briefly feel her pain because, in spite of her initial fear, she managed to develop a love for expressing herself through words, as well as art.

MESSAGES FROM SAM: Although art, music, and dance are huge areas of creative expression for Sam, her soul also has a great passion for writing. When she first mentioned this, she also confirmed that she had enjoyed writing when she was here. "I wrote stories," she announced. She continued by bragging that she could have been published had she lived longer.[3]

On one occasion, Sam introduced herself to a medium as a "very creative" spirit and then sent an image of herself writing.[4] A couple of months later, with a different medium, Sam revealed that her passion for creating stories was present from an early age. However, she didn't actually start writing them until age nine or ten. She admitted that she got better in her mid-teens. She reaffirmed her previous statement about her writing ability: "I was good enough that I would have eventually been published."[5]

In addition, Sam has brought up the inspiration she channels, or sends, down here in the area of writing. Just as she sometimes inspires people to create music and art, she inspires people here with ideas for books, movies, and plays. Once she proudly stated she had given ideas for book trilogies.[6] It brings me joy to hear that she is sharing her talents with so many.

When boasting about her ability to write, Sam slipped in the idea of me carrying on her energy in this area. "You have this version of a story, and I want you to take it as far

---

3. SH, October 2017
4. KB, August 8, 2018
5. JD, October 5, 2018
6. JD, August 6, 2020

as you can go."[7] *This came a few months after she surprised me with a similar message. I had just asked her about one of my health issues. "Don't worry," she said teasingly. "They don't want you upstairs yet. You still have things to do right here on earth." Then she spelled out W-R-I-T-E to replace the word* right *and added, "You still have things to write about here on earth."*[8]

Since that message, Sam has urged me numerous times, through several mediums, to write. This mission seems extremely important to her.[9] And when I think back on one of our first conversations following her passing, I recall her telling me that she and I would be working on a project together, and she would help me to help others. But she wouldn't tell me what it was.[10] I'm guessing she didn't want to intimidate me with the mention of writing a book.

Recently, my guides and Sam finally admitted that they purposely didn't encourage me to actually write this book until this past year, four years after Sam's passing. They knew it would have been too overwhelming for me any sooner. This is so true. I would have both laughed and cried had they wanted me to write a book soon after Sam's death. They reiterated that the desire had to come from me.[11]

Sam said the greatest part about the writing is my growth and healing. Knowing that I want to share it means I have healed a great deal. Sam revealed that before we came into this life, we decided that she would work on this book with me from the other side. Therefore, it's one of her missions, as well as mine.[12]

---

7. SH, October 2017
8. GK, March 2, 2017
9. MH, May 9, 2017; SH, 2017; JD, August 1, 2018; JD, September 21, 2018; SH, January 30, 2019; JD, June 15, 2019; MG, November 1, 2019; JD, February 6, 2020
10. GK, November 16, 2015
11. JD, February 6, 2020
12. MG, November 1, 2019

Falling with Grace

When Sam was between the ages of four and six, I taught art to children at home. By this point, Sam wasn't holding back from expressing her creative side, and she didn't want or need much guidance from me. She would listen to my instructions regarding materials with which she had no previous experience, but she was on her own during my classes. Our unspoken agreement was that I would do my thing and she would do hers, as long as it didn't interfere with my teaching the other students. Sam was well behaved, mostly. Because of her creative confidence and the fact that she was at home, Sam felt extremely comfortable in my class.

One day before class, Sam lured a couple of students upstairs to play in her room. I was busy with last-minute preparations and greeting incoming students. At the start of class, I called out to Sam and the others. The staircase was right outside the art room, so it didn't take long for the students to come down. Sam, however, did not come with them.

I continued to call out to her, in an increasingly firm tone. Eventually, I heard her bounding down the hallway above me and starting down the stairs.

Then I heard something terrifying. There were several loud bangs as Sam fell all the way down the stairs and hit the hardwood floor at the bottom. My heart stopped.

I whirled around to see Sam lying still on the floor. It was obvious from the position and the sound of her skull hitting the floor that she had fallen headfirst. I knew there was a good chance that she had broken her neck and was dead. And if she wasn't dead, she was badly injured. Panic engulfed me.

But before I could get to her, Sam rolled over and popped up. I couldn't speak; I was shocked but extremely grateful. She didn't even cry, and she wasn't injured—in any way. I knew at that moment that someone had intervened and protected her.

MESSAGES FROM SAM: During three different conversations, Sam confirmed that when she was young, she fell down a whole flight of stairs at our house. Showing herself around the age of four or five, she demonstrated losing her footing while playing around. Sam explained that one of her angels had wrapped her in protection and she had no injuries.[1]

This event happened in a period of Sam's life when it wasn't an option for her to depart. It wasn't her time. And thankfully, her angels chose to protect her completely, preventing any kind of injury.

But what does "it wasn't her time" really mean? Sam and my other guides have attempted to clarify this.

Exit Points

Before we come into a human life, we choose the approximate time we want to leave. And we usually pick more than one point in time. These planned departures are called "exit points." Although rare, we have the option to not have any. And even if we do have planned exit points, as humans, we can end our lives if we choose—because of free will.[2] *If we make it to our last exit point, that's it. It's over. We're*

---

1. JD, September 7, 2018; SH, January 30, 2019; JD, February 22, 2019
2. JD, May 28, 2020; JD, February 18, 2020

leaving. Sam's life was always meant to end early. But fortunately, she stayed until her last exit point.

The reason we might have more than one exit point is because it increases our chances of fulfilling our purpose. If we don't take one of the first exit points it is because we know on a soul level that we haven't done, or learned, everything we planned. And if an opportunity to leave comes too early, angels can intervene. This often happens if the event would be catastrophic.[3]

My curiosity got the better of me during my most recent discussion with Sam about exit points. I unwisely inquired about my possible times to leave. Now, first let me say that as far as I've been told, spirits on the other side do not offer the time a person is going to die. However, Sam decided to inform me that at this stage of my life, I still have three exit points remaining.

Wow! *I thought.* How many did I start off with? And what kinds of disasters or illnesses will I suffer through if my soul doesn't think I should leave until the last one? *Sam said if I make it to the last one, I will be very old and wrinkled.*[4] *For me, that wasn't comforting news. I've already got wrinkles.*

---

3. JD, February 18, 2020
4. JD, May 28, 2020

Missed Our Exit

During Sam's early childhood years, I drove a small, jeep-like SUV. It was compact but tall, and its height made it unstable in strong winds. In many instances, it just didn't feel heavy enough to remain upright.

After running errands on the far side of town one day, when Sam was about seven, I drove the two of us home via a major highway. It was raining when we got on the road. I didn't like driving in bad weather, and my concern about the wind made me nervous. I was also worried about my tires, which were getting worn down.

Although the rain was light, it had just begun, so oil would be floating on the surface. From my experience, this was the worst time for not-so-good tires to be on a highway. I kept my anxiety at bay as the mild rain turned into a blinding downpour. There were cars all around me driving at high speeds, but I couldn't see them. At one point, I tried to slow down, but when I touched the brakes, the car started hydroplaning. Within seconds, we were fishtailing and sliding from left to right.

Then we started to spin. I knew that our lives were either over or we were going to be severely injured, which I considered a much worse fate.

Temporarily, I couldn't see anything. Feeling the SUV's frightening movements, I braced myself for the inevitable impact with another car. My mind went blank. What seemed like a second later, I felt the vehicle moving forward again. The rain had lessened, and I could now see. We were in our lane and the nightmare was over. I was both stunned and elated.

I knew at that moment that Sam and I had received divine help. Without it, there was no way we could have avoided a horrific accident.

MESSAGES FROM SAM: The first time Cecil, my main guide, introduced himself, he brought up the car accident I had avoided twenty years prior. He took full credit for saving our lives.[1] *He said it was an opportunity for both Sam and me to exit but that neither of us were ready to go. If we both left, I wouldn't have fulfilled my mission of experiencing the loss of a child. Sam added, "I was always going to go young." However, if Sam had departed at that time, it would have been too early for her to accomplish all she had planned.*[2]

Two years after Cecil acknowledged his role in saving us from the car accident, I asked Sam if she could recall that experience. I had never asked her about it when she was here, and I'm not sure why. Perhaps I didn't want to bring up something that would be frightening or confusing to her. She informed me that she was aware of the experience as it happened but that she wasn't afraid, as I had been. She could see and feel everything, which included the car spinning.[3] *She said the car did a complete 360 before it straightened out, but time had slowed down, so she wasn't frightened. The non-jarring movements kept her calm. She could see the outside world moving in slow motion. Sam added that people in nearby cars would have seen our car spin in real time.*[4]

---

1. JD, August 17, 2018
2. JD, February 18, 2020
3. JD, August 6, 2020
4. JD, December 3, 2020

Saved by the Belt

Although Sam had realized her gifts for creating art at the young age of two, it was several years before she found success in a physical activity.

When she was in her last year of preschool, I enrolled Sam in ballet lessons taught by a good friend of mine. Sam resisted a little, but I had hoped that she'd enjoy them once they started. She didn't. After a few weeks, I apologized to my friend, who politely suggested Sam should drop out. To this day, I regret ever putting Sam in that position. I can only imagine her withdrawing more and more as the lessons progressed. The class hadn't been open to viewing. If it had been, I might have seen Sam's frustration and pulled her out sooner.

MESSAGES FROM SAM: From the other side, Sam has brought up her love for dance many times—ballet included. During one discussion, she also expressed her affinity for ballet costumes and provided an image of herself wearing a tutu. She followed this visual aid with the acknowledgment that her apparent dislike for ballet classes as a child had more to do with being "oppositional" to my wishes. She didn't dislike it as much as she let on. Once, she told a medium, "Sometimes, if my mother really loved something, I was a little difficult."

However, she did confirm her love of dancing while she

was here. She felt a sense of freedom when she was dancing or singing.[1]

It's comforting to know that Sam's soul loves to dance, especially since it's one of my passions.[2] *She has brought up several past lives where both she and I were dancers.*[3] *But she pointed out that I had been more drawn to ballet than she had.*[4]

Now that Sam is on the other side, there are endless opportunities for her to dance.[5] *And it's not uncommon for her to express her lively, fun-loving nature by dancing during our conversations.*[6] *Once, she tap-danced in with a cane, as if she were entering the stage in a musical.*[7]

By kindergarten, Sam was hearing about the many interests of her classmates and friends but hadn't yet asked to participate in anything other than art. Sam was very secure with her artistic abilities and she spent most of her time indoors, expressing her creativity.

However, she did seem enthusiastic when we signed her up for our town's soccer program. As parents who supported lifelong physical activity, we were delighted. In addition, we had learned from Sam's pediatric checkups that she had a slow metabolism and needed to be more physical.

It was during the soccer lessons that a behavior pattern came to light. As early as age two, I had noticed something peculiar about Sam when she played with other children. Throughout her preschool years, Sam enjoyed going to playgrounds and meeting up with her school friends. I enjoyed the play dates as much as she did. Maybe more, especially

---

1. JD, December 11, 2018
2. JD, February 7, 2019
3. JD, April 30, 2020
4. JD, February 7, 2019
5. JD, August 31, 2019
6. JF, September 7, 2016; BH, April 27, 2017; BH, Early 2018; JD, October 11, 2018; JD, June 15, 2020
7. JD, March 5, 2020

since I had become close friends with the mothers of two of Sam's schoolmates.

At first, Sam would play with the others. But as soon as they started doing something that intimidated her, like hanging from the monkey bars or climbing the ladder of a tall slide, she would wander outside the playground. Often, she would occupy herself by picking weeds and grass. I eventually had to corral her back. I did my best to encourage interaction with her friends, without pushing her to do something she didn't want to do.

One of Sam's friends was so physically gifted that I could foresee her becoming a professional athlete one day. She would try anything, without fear. Meanwhile, Sam would withdraw and only rarely attempt new things. I got the impression that she believed her friends had had some sort of playground training.

When Sam began soccer, this behavior continued. She was placed in a large group of kids her age. Unfortunately, she'd never played soccer, as most of the others had. From the start, she was intimidated by their skills, and I presumed her embarrassment kept her from really trying. Not long after the lessons began, I would see her wandering around, focusing on anything but soccer. She soon lost interest and didn't want to go back. Not wanting to reinforce quitting, her father and I strongly suggested she stick it out for the rest of the lessons. Some days I felt it was more painful for me to watch Sam show up and barely participate than it was for her to be there.

After dance and soccer came gymnastics and tennis. The pattern was always the same: Sam was too intimidated to try what the other children appeared to already know how to do. I would drag her to lessons she no longer wanted to take.

In second grade, she joined a T-ball league. And although she stayed committed for two, maybe three, entire seasons, she would lose interest in the middle of each game. The coach wisely placed her in an outfield position that wasn't close to the bases. Rarely did a ball ever reach Sam, which worked out well since she was usually more interested in finding things on the ground.

Sam's insecurities went beyond physical activities as well. In third grade, at the age of eight, Sam felt tortured by the other girls in her class. Later, she would refer to third grade as one of her worst school years. This particular class disproportionately consisted of physically mature girls who were obsessed with fashion, self-image, and the opposite sex. Sam had more interest in the world of Pokémon. Her obsession with the Pokémon card game, TV shows, and the adorable creatures evoked ridicule from these boy-crazy classmates.

But during this unpleasant school year, two of Sam's friends, who were brothers and lived a few houses up the street, began taking taekwondo classes. When they showed off their skills to Sam, she became intrigued and eventually hooked. Their mother and I took turns driving the three to lessons a couple of days a week. I'm not sure if Sam's initial interest was the result of finding something that fit her personality, or if she just wanted to impress the kids at school. Regardless, her confidence soared. She had finally found a physical activity that made her feel accomplished and proud of her efforts. Thankfully, with that discovery, her self-confidence increased significantly. This new confidence nudged her into opening up socially. And all of this brought me great relief.

By fourth grade, Sam was doing well in both school and taekwondo. At ten, she earned her first-degree black belt

(junior level). And by age twelve, she had her second-degree black belt.

MESSAGES FROM SAM: When I asked Sam about her third-grade class, she responded, "I just didn't like the people."[8] *She also confessed that her anxiety contributed to the agony of that year.*[9]

---
8. SH, January 30, 2019
9. JD, February 7, 2019

I'm so grateful Sam succeeded in taekwondo. Before that, I had been confused as to whether her challenges were due to the intimidation of trying new things or because she wasn't as coordinated as the average child. However, recently she acknowledged that both insecurity and fear of hurting herself held her back. But she blamed her free-spirited nature for causing her to wander off during activities. She admitted that she would have preferred to be doing something else.[10] *She also stressed that there were so many things she could have done, and if she had known what she now knows, she would have tried everything when she was here.*[11]

In addition, Sam confessed that self-consciousness played a part in her not wanting to try the physical feats that her friends could do. She said it was more severe than anybody realized. "Even when I was young, if people were talking, I would be worried they were talking about me." She continued, "I have worked through so much of that from over here. But that's something I planned to come in and work on. I was really very self-conscious there this time."[12]

---

10. JD, July 23, 2020
11. JD, October 5, 2018
12. JD, December 11, 2018

A Big Deal

When Sam was in first grade, David and I ended our marriage. We had faced the typical challenges in our marriage that most couples do, and perhaps a few unique struggles. After seventeen years, we conceded to divorce.

I imagine David blamed the failure of our marriage on my health problems, and if so, I believe that his assessment was partially correct. My health provided challenges that few relationships would have survived. It's conceivable that a stronger love could have endured. It is also possible that had we taken a different course and not married each other, my physical problems might have been different, lessened, or nonexistent.

Whether we started off as a good fit or not, several issues contributed to our downfall. Through the years, I could see our differences growing. Raising Sam kept us together for a while. With a common goal of providing the love and security of a family-centered childhood, we managed to operate as a successful parenting team for several years.

As far as I could tell, the divorce didn't significantly affect Sam. We took our time working out the details, and David tried to make the separation more of an adventure for Sam than a loss. He found a nice apartment with a playground, and they made friends there with a family who had a young daughter. We stressed the "twice as much fun" aspect of divorce (two Christmases, birthdays, etc.).

By the time Sam had finished elementary school, David was remarried and had started another family. As an only child, Sam was thrilled to have siblings. A couple of years following the birth of their first child, David and his wife decided to move to another state. Sam then spent alternating holidays and four weeks in the summer with them. At first, I felt out of sorts when she was away. I missed her, and our home felt lifeless. But I took the opportunity to visit friends, date, and work on unfinished projects.

Upon entering middle school, Sam became more focused on social life. She no longer felt the need to take taekwondo classes. Art, schoolwork, and friends were her main interests. And sometime during the latter part of middle school, Sam developed a romantic relationship with Robert, a schoolmate and neighbor.

Having a low metabolism, her body needed regular exercise, but by this age, it was obvious Sam would rather be inside drawing than exerting physical energy. She also expressed that she felt sick when she got overheated.

It wasn't until college that Sam shared with me her inability to sweat like the average person. Since her passing, I have learned that not being able to sweat is extremely dangerous. There are moments that I rack my brain trying to remember any moment of her of life when she glistened with sweat. I can't. But I can recall her face getting horribly flushed in hot weather.

MESSAGES FROM SAM: I had a lot of guilt about not identifying her inability to sweat. When I apologized to Sam about this, she comforted me, saying, "It's fine." But she described how red she would get from overheating as a child. And she said there really wasn't a whole lot that could have been done. "Eventually, I got to a point where I could sweat. And that helped."[1]

---

1. JD, November 9, 2018

During her middle school and high school summers, Sam spent a week at a camp sponsored by the Episcopal Church. Physical games were included in the daily activities, but they were not the focus. However, every summer, by the end of the camp session, Sam had grown emotionally, socially, and spiritually.

Unfortunately, she slowly put on weight from the lack of routine exercise. Every time she visited her father, he criticized her about it. She dreaded visiting him because of this. Her weight inevitably increased before each visit, and her self-image would drastically decline afterward.

Sam's appearance and lack of confidence also affected her relationship with Robert, who had a smaller frame and was more fit. The two dated off and on throughout the end of middle school and four years of high school.

MESSAGES FROM SAM: Sam acknowledged her weight problem here and admitted that no matter how hard she tried, she could never have the body she wanted. She felt like she was born in the wrong body.[2]

Regarding her relationship with her dad, Sam said he could have learned more from her than he actually did. There were many missed opportunities. However, he did learn from her passing.[3]

Sam's weight issue was a lesson mostly intended for her, but it was for others, too. She says lessons are almost never for just one person. Compassion, sympathy, and acceptance were what others could learn from her weight problem. In retrospect, it seems obvious that compassion and acceptance were lessons that Sam's weight offered her dad.

As for Sam, part of her learning from this focused on not having control. She had many lives as a fit, beautiful, and desirable person. She confessed, "[I had] a lifetime where I did pick on other people for being heavy." So, she chose to

---

2. BH, Early 2018
3. JD, September 21, 2018

come here and experience the opposite side of that issue. She adds that some issues here might appear small to us, but in the spiritual world they could be a "big deal." She stressed that being a heavy person is considered a big deal and it only seems insignificant until you are experiencing it.[4]

---

4. JD, June 15, 2020

Two Peas in a Pod

Sam's passion for art had always been evident, but it wasn't until middle school that Sam demonstrated an interest in math. She joined the math club in eighth grade and thrived on the recognition from her friends and family. I believe the validation of her analytical abilities enticed her to join the math club in high school, and to stay in it for all four years.

MESSAGES FROM SAM: A creative being, Sam often uses imagery to get her point across. To illustrate her connection with math, Sam has flashed math symbols during sessions with different mediums. Some of the symbols weren't even recognizable as ones we use here.[1]

I worried about Sam's self-confidence during her middle school and high school years. Her self-image continued to decline as she continued to gain weight. But being a member of the math club was a boost to her ego, and it also provided a new group of friends. Overall, I felt good about her involvement. However, math clubs are about math competitions, at which Sam did not always perform well. She was not one of the stars.

It has occurred to me that Sam's efforts to stay in the club during those high school years might have been partially driven by a desire to impress her father. I suspected

---
1. BH, April 27, 2017; KB, August 8, 2018

that Sam hoped he would notice her intellectual abilities because he didn't seem to value her creative ones.

MESSAGES FROM SAM: Sam's intellectual capability was as evident as her artistic talent. Mediums have described her as being a bright and intelligent young woman when she was here and as a smart, wise, brilliant, high-functioning, cerebral, and knowledgeable being on the other side.[2]

Sam delivers her messages with the wisdom of a soul who has been around for eons. And whenever she concludes a serious or technical message, she always slips back into her playful mode: "I know more than you think I do. I'm sort of wise beyond my years."[3] *This is amusing to me because whenever she appears, Sam looks to be in her late twenties.*

Her father lectured Sam about the importance of a career other than art. I believe this was a result of being married to me. During our college years, David was impressed with my work ethic and success in my design courses. Unfortunately, I didn't make much money in any area of art after we were married.

Perhaps my encouragement and constant support countered the pressure Sam felt from her father. She loved animation and decided to make it her primary career goal. I was proud of her for standing up for her dream.

MESSAGES FROM SAM: Around the age of eight, Sam began internalizing all the negative comments from her father. From what Sam shared with me while she was alive, most of his statements concentrated on her appearance. Her increasing weight and blemished skin were constant issues. However, David did lecture her on other topics, such

---

2. JF, September 7, 2016; GK, October 17, 2016; BH, April 27, 2017; SH, January 10, 2018; SH, January 30, 2019; JD, March 7, 2019
3. SH, October 2017

as work ethic and having a financially secure vocation.

I believe David criticized Sam in hopes of teaching her, and therefore making her a better person—from his perspective. I'm confident his intentions came from a place of love. A year after her passing, Sam acknowledged that her dad hadn't understood her.[4] *But she has also defended him. "He's a decent guy. He has a lot of struggles."*[5]

Fortunately, Sam knows I was "her biggest fan." When she was alive, she knew I encouraged and supported her in everything.[6] *"You always believed in me."*[7] *At least three times, Sam conveyed her appreciation for the way I allowed her to be her own person—that I trusted her and let her express her own personality.*[8]

Having a brain that excels in both math and art isn't that unusual, but it felt like more than a coincidence that she and I had this in common. Not wanting Sam to feel more insecure about areas she didn't do well in, I tried not to talk much about my past accomplishments with her. However, I'm sure she picked up on the fact that art and math were my strong suits. Certainly, my being both a math and an art teacher must have been a clue.

I've often wondered if Sam invested energy in math to be like me. I hope not. It always bothered me that we both loved the same disciplines but she never wanted my input. It took all I had as a mother and a teacher to honor her wishes. When she absolutely needed assistance, she called on a classmate.

Why did Sam and I have the same interests? Was it a coincidence? On some level, did she want to be like me? Are

---

4. SH, October 3, 2016
5. JD, September 21, 2018
6. SH, January 10, 2018; KB, August 8, 2018; JD, September 3, 2020
7. JF, September 7, 2016
8. SH, October 3, 2016; BH, Early 2018; JD, August 17, 2018

art and math in both of our human genetic makeups? Or were they spiritual similarities that came with us into this life?

MESSAGES FROM SAM: Sam has repeatedly revealed that our souls have similar characteristics and interests. In addition to our artistic abilities, we both are free-spirited and adventurous,[9] and we have a tremendous love of animals.[10] Interestingly, but not surprisingly, Sam has also confirmed that math is a part of her soul, as well as mine.[11] She said that for her, math and art are connected.[12]

I asked Sam why she didn't let me teach or help her with art and math. She gave different reasons for each. She explained that with her art, she wanted it to be completely hers. Even if I didn't actually touch her work—which I would never do—my energy would be part of it. As for the math, she said my attempts at helping her wouldn't have been effective because they would have created anxiety, and then she would have shut down. She didn't understand it at the time, but it was the right decision for the two of us. And she revealed, "It was part of our plan." But then she said, "You gave me so much more in other areas."[13]

Sam's intelligence didn't shine in school as much as it could have. I believe this is because she didn't spend a reasonable amount of energy and time studying. However, she did take some challenging advanced courses and had to apply herself at times. But she didn't have to expend much energy to earn As in all her art and computer art courses.

Fortunately, Sam had an outstanding teacher in her three years of computer art, which added to her self-confidence

---

9. GK, October 12, 2017; SH, January 30, 2019; JD, August 1, 2019; JD, November 18, 2019
10. JD, November 18, 2019
11. JD, October 5, 2018; JD, September 3, 2020
12. JD, October 5, 2018
13. JD, October 5, 2018

going into the study of animation. I wish I could say the same regarding her art teacher. As an art teacher myself, I watched Sam miss an opportunity to learn basic drawing techniques and composition, which would have given her a solid foundation for her future.

In one way, I'm relieved that she didn't devote excessive time to schoolwork. She thrived on creating art or writing stories, and her projects motivated her. If I think back on her entire short life, I feel relief knowing that she spent a great deal of time creating. She was a true artist. And her spirit intuitively knew to continually express itself and share her gift.

MESSAGES FROM SAM: Sam acknowledged my concern for her to do well in school. As a spirit, she understands that I just wanted her to feel good about herself and to have more opportunities in her future. She has expressed her gratitude for the freedom I gave her in choosing the amount of effort she devoted to school. She also admitted that I knew she had more important things to do, and that I was very understanding. "There were other things I would rather be doing." Of course, art was at the top of the list.[14]

---

14. JD, March 7, 2019

The Stolen Years

A few months after David and I divorced, I met Jake. I remember our first date vividly. We went to the movies. During the drive to the theater, he talked a lot about past relationships. I sensed his insecurity and thought the evening would be a bust.

Before the movie, we chatted and got to know each other a little better. By the time the show was over, I had begun enjoying myself. Leaving the theater, I recall turning a corner of the building and getting a message in my head. It was so clear: *Hang in there with this guy.* And I did. For four years.

Before long, Jake appeared to be smitten with me. And although we didn't have much in common, I reveled in the attention he gave me. He and David were complete opposites.

As a couple, Jake and I confused my friends and family. Because of his insecure and sometimes immature behavior, everyone could see we weren't a match. At first, I didn't mind what others thought. He showered me with all the compliments and attention that I had craved for two decades.

By the time we had fallen in love, I was only just beginning to learn who Jake really was. Our relationship became tumultuous. Life was fun, when it wasn't interrupted by his erratic, childish behavior.

As a whole, Sam didn't experience the negatives. Mostly,

Jake treated her with kindness, but there were a few times when he was belittling and mean.

For years after breaking up with Jake, I berated myself for the times I allowed his needs to take precedence over Sam's. Occasionally, Sam would say something that I recognized as a cry for attention. And if Jake didn't like it, sometimes he would scold her. Other times, he would ignore her and monopolize my time. When I reflect on particular incidences, I realize why I didn't give Sam my attention—I was protecting myself from Jake's disturbing reactions. I wish I could have been stronger and spoken up more often.

During the last year of our relationship, I was emotionally drained. I was falling out of love with Jake, and he could sense this. So, he started to take more of an interest in Sam. He would plan special creative activities with her, which she loved. And although I knew why he was doing this, I went along with it. It felt good to see Sam receiving fatherly attention.

Just as I had in the beginning of our relationship, I received a divine message near the end. It came at Christmas, which has always been a special time for Sam and me. And whenever Sam spent Christmas with her father, I felt an emptiness. But fortunately for Sam, she was at her father's that year. Otherwise, Jake's behavior might have ruined her Christmas at home.

It was Christmas Eve and I had planned to go to church. Before I left for the service, Jake lectured me about something I had said to him earlier. He was furious, even though I wasn't aware of having said anything wrong.

Later, in church, as I stood in a long line waiting to approach the altar for communion, in my head I heard the encouraging words, *Next Christmas will be different.*

It was just a week or two after that Christmas Eve message that I met my prince.

MESSAGES FROM SAM: Throughout our lives, we are told we learn from our mistakes. But it has taken me most of my life to truly accept that all my bad experiences hold value. Until now, I presumed the lessons were meant to assist us in this life. Now, I know that they do so much more. Every experience, good or bad, has the potential to strengthen our spiritual growth both here and in the hereafter.[1]

I asked Sam if she was able to forgive me, when she was alive, for the times I put Jake's needs first. She replied that at the time she was upset, but she now understands why I did it. She said he had me confused. I wasn't sure what he would do, and I needed to protect us. She acknowledged that I finally found the strength to end the relationship and that I have worried far too much about how it affected her.

Even though I would have preferred to suppress my memories of my time with Jake, Sam said it was important for me to write about that period. I used to look at those four years with Jake as a time in my life that was stolen from Sam and me. One day, I will understand all the good that came from it.

Sam's final words on this matter: "You learned a lot from him."[2]

---

1. JD, July 2, 2019
2. JD, September 21, 2018

Meeting Max

At the beginning of January 2002, I decided to throw Jake a surprise birthday party. As strange as it may seem, I wanted to hold a special event that included his family and friends to remind him that there were others who cared about him. I knew that I needed to end our relationship soon, and in my mind, this was the best gift I could give him.

I decided to host the party at a popular Italian restaurant that Jake and I enjoyed. One Saturday, Sam and I had lunch, without Jake, at the restaurant. My mission was to enjoy a nice lunch with Sam and to gather information for hosting the party.

A hugely successful operation, the restaurant was often filled to capacity. That day was no exception. When we entered, we were greeted by a friendly man in his late thirties, whose attire suggested that he was a manager of some sort. And although I believe a hostess was in the vicinity, he stepped forward to assist us.

I took the opportunity to mention that we were not only there for lunch, but I wanted to speak with someone about planning a party. He quickly responded by saying he could help me, and then he led us to a quiet booth. Sam sat next to me.

After introducing himself as Max, this attentive manager left to retrieve catering information while a server took our order. When Max returned to our table, he sat down across from us and chatted a while. His warm and enthusiastic demeanor captured my attention.

Before our entrées arrived, a large salad bowl—from which we could serve ourselves—was brought to our table. This salad has been the subject of many conversations over the years. Max swears that I ate lettuce directly out of this large serving bowl while talking to him. I do not remember this and have continued to deny it for eighteen years. Max believes that I must have been so attracted to him that I was unaware of what I was doing.

During the conversation, I informed Max that the party was for my boyfriend. I felt compelled, for some reason, to say that we wouldn't be together much longer. At this point, I didn't see Max as a potential romantic interest. I wasn't sure if he was flirting with me or just selling the party. For all I knew, he could have been married. Before leaving, he used "we" to describe where he and his family lived. I felt a twinge of disappointment. I later learned that he and his wife were separated and working on a divorce; the "we" referred to his children and him.

After the meal, Max walked us to the parking lot. I vaguely remember him pulling additional menu information out of the trunk of his car and handing it to me, then he escorted us to my car. I believe he offered this additional information as an excuse to walk with us, although he denies it. Now we're even.

Before leaving the restaurant, Max had informed me that he was the general manager. I later learned that he rarely spent time planning events; he just happened to be at the front of the restaurant when we walked in.

Months later, Max shared with me a conversation he had with a cashier later that day. She had asked who I was. "My girlfriend," he replied. Surprised, the cashier asked why he hadn't introduced me. Then, with his occasional cocky attitude, he replied, "She doesn't know it yet."

From my perspective, the party for Jake was a disappointment. I had hoped Max would be working that night, but he wasn't. The servers weren't at their best, and some of Jake's family were disrespectful. However,ced the evening. And that's what mattered most.

During the next few months, I ran into Max a couple more times at the restaurant. On one of these occasions, Sam and I were meeting Jake, who was running late. Before Jake arrived, Max came by our table. It was now clear that he hadn't been simply trying to sell us the party during our first encounter, because he was obviously interested in me.

Sam immediately became protective of Jake, who had successfully won her acceptance with his attention over the past few months. She rudely asked me, "Are you flirting?"

Max politely responded with a smile, "No, I was flirting with her." And then he asked for my phone number.

What I did next still haunts me. In a packed dining room, I blurted out in a louder-than-usual voice, "I thought you were married."

This apparently pleased him immensely. He heard passion and interest in my tone. I was so embarrassed—people at the nearby tables were staring. Quietly, I let him know that we were waiting on someone.

The next time I saw him, he and his two daughters were shopping at my favorite grocery store. I saw him first but didn't say anything. He looked different. I saw vulnerability in him. He and his girls had come from an outing at a public swimming pool, and he was dressed casually. I also saw that one of his children had special needs. I could only imagine the life he lived outside of the hectic restaurant world.

When he saw me, he lit up. I acted surprised.

This brief encounter changed everything for me. Max bravely asked for my phone number again. I paused and then decided to give him my work number. It seemed safer, especially since I hadn't yet succeeded in completely severing my relationship with Jake.

MESSAGES FROM SAM: Sam said my relationship with Max in this life was preplanned.[1] And to my amazement, he and I have had several lives together.[2] Knowing more about my connection to Max now, our eventual meeting and attraction makes sense.

Although we've had children together in other lives, it hasn't happened often. In one life, we lost a child, a son. He died of an illness similar to dysentery. According to Sam, this is one of the reasons we didn't meet earlier in this life and have any children together. It brings up a painful soul memory.[3]

It took several months after hearing the reassuring Christmas Eve message for me to end the relationship with Jake. And even after Max and I began dating, there were still a few frightening moments with Jake. He had difficulty accepting our breakup. One evening, when Max was visiting me at home, Jake dropped by. He attempted to barge in when I answered the door. In a loud and angry tone, he announced his intent to confront Max. With as much force as I could muster, I pushed him out.

That night was the beginning of the end. Although I had several civil chats with Jake soon after, he finally got the message we were officially over. Max and I dated for about two years, juggling single-parent activities and obligations. And then his ex-wife asked for custody of the children. Up until that point, she hadn't wanted the responsibility. With deep sadness and disappointment, Max decided not to fight her. He knew that unless proven unfit, a mother would win custody.

He asked me to marry him several months after his children moved out of his house. Three months later, we were married. He moved in with Sam and me.

---

1. JD, December 10, 2019
2. BH, Early 2018; JD, September 7, 2018
3. JD, January 21, 2020

MESSAGES FROM SAM: More than once, Sam has stated that Max and I are not soulmates. However, we are more than "acquaintances." We know each other well and hang out on the other side.[4]

This baffles me. In addition to losing a child together, we've had twenty-seven lives together. Although most weren't romantic, I would have thought that we'd have formed a much stronger bond by now.[5]

Out of curiosity, I asked Sam one day whether my guides and Max's guides communicate with each other when we argue or disagree. Her response was amusing, as she attempted to describe the conversation: "Okay. Now, if he would just do this, and she could just do this... If he could see that this is what she means when she says this..."[6] So, I guess they do chat among themselves. And hopefully, we entertain them sometimes.

---

4. JD, March 29, 2019
5. JD, August 17, 2018
6. JD, December 10, 2019

My Hero

In 2004, a few weeks before our wedding, Max and his good friend Pete took over a failing country club restaurant in the small town of Cairo, Georgia. It was only a forty-five minute drive from where we lived in Florida. The two made a great team and quickly became successful. The club members loved the food and the good service provided by the cute young waitresses.

At this time, I was working at Florida State University as an administrative assistant. It was a stressful job that exposed me to many irritants. Needing a healthier work environment, I gladly left my job to help at the restaurant. I handled all the accounting and supervised the set-up of the banquet room for meetings and weddings. Honestly, it was the best job I've ever had. It was flexible, part-time, and I had the best bosses ever.

But at the end of the restaurant's second year, I injured my right leg. While cleaning at home, I squatted too quickly and aggravated a muscle below my knee. This type of muscle injury was a frequent occurrence for me, and I usually recovered in a few days. However, the pain continued to get worse as I tried to massage the problem away. By the next day, I was unable to walk. It took weeks to get the not-so-specific diagnosis that I had torn tissue in my knee.

For the next two months, I sat at home in an overstuffed chair. By this time, my sensitivity to chemicals had increased to a level that caused me to react to almost all medications, including anti-inflammatories like ibuprofen. But without something to bring the swelling down, the injury got worse before it got better. And while most people would have healed from this in a few weeks, my recovery was long and drawn out.

Due to my fibromyalgia, any muscle injury I sustained became a complicated issue with long-lasting consequences. Because I didn't have the muscle strength to use crutches, I decided to try using a walker. After a few days, my wrists became so aggravated from bearing my own weight that I caused serious injury to them as well. I could no longer walk or use my hands.

Max became my hero. I thank God that he's unusually strong and I'm of average size because every day before going to work, Max would carry me downstairs to my comfy chair and ottoman and leave the TV remote along with plenty of food and water next to me. He also made sure that there was easy-to-grab food in the fridge. Lucky for me, our downstairs bathroom and the kitchen were close by, and I was able to hop to them. Sam, a sophomore in high school during this time, would also get things for me when she returned home from school each day.

At night, Max would prepare dinner, carry me upstairs, help me bathe, and put me in bed. I can't imagine the burden my condition put on him, and helping me bathe must have been the worst of it for him. It sure was for me. There were a few weeks where I couldn't even hold soap, much less scrub. To make matters worse, I was sitting naked in the tub, with a body that was becoming less and less fit, while he still had his clothes on. Humiliating, to say the least.

I also couldn't use my laptop. Even pushing the touch pad caused pain. That really sent me over the edge. Otherwise, I could have been playing online poker every day, instead of just watching TV. Perhaps I could have become a great poker player. Maybe in another life.

Since the leg and hand injuries I suffered fourteen years

ago, I've learned to be extremely cautious. Even now, I'm constantly straining the muscles in my legs and reinjuring my wrists. Turning door handles is difficult some days. And I won't ever jog again. However, I'm very grateful to be able to walk.

MESSAGES FROM SAM: *I asked Sam what she experienced during those weeks I sat in that chair, unable to be her mother. Sam said she hated that time in our lives. It was a sad time for her. "My routine was not any different than it usually was, except that there was so much fear and anxiety."*

She would bring me things, like food or books, when I asked for them. But she explained to the medium, "In no way was I waiting on her." Following this statement, Sam flashed an image of our two-story house and then showed herself upstairs doing homework while I remained downstairs. Fortunately, by this time, she could basically take care of herself.

Sam added, "I did not understand what was actually going on." She felt like Max and I were keeping something from her. She worried that my condition was worse than we let on. Although I, too, had felt concern over the extent of my injuries, I wish I'd had the foresight to reassure her that my condition was only temporary.

For me, this was a reminder that parents sometimes go overboard trying to protect their children from tragedies and turmoil. In the end, it might have been healthier for me to include Sam in a few of the discussions about my injuries.

When I thanked Sam for sharing her thoughts on this unpleasant time, she cheered up and said, "You're welcome." Then she bent forward and, circling her hand several times, gave me a grand theatrical bow. She really enjoys lightening the mood with cute gestures. And like always, it worked. I laughed.[1]

---
1. JD, April 12, 2019

Sensitive Subject

By the time Sam was in the latter part of middle school, my sensitivities to other people's care products (fragrances, detergents, shampoos, and deodorants) had become so severe that she could no longer bring her friends home. I felt terribly guilty about this.

I believe the decline in my condition resulted from a combination of being exposed to harmful products at work and taking too many antibiotics. I often developed bacterial infections when I caught someone else's virus and would become too sick to heal without medicine.

Fortunately, my mother offered her sunporch and my deceased stepfather's workshop for Sam's parties and get-togethers. Though I felt as if I were letting her down, the situation worked out great for her, with no parents hanging around. And I only had to help with refreshments. A win-win for both of us.

I specifically remember shopping for decorations with Sam for her eighteenth birthday party and then setting them up on my mother's porch. At this point in time, I had reactions in every store I entered. Surviving the various chemicals from the products and people in the party store was difficult, but I cherish the fun we had together.

Almost every encounter with Sam's high school friends astonished me. They were understanding and seemed to be aware of my restrictions and limitations. I felt comfort in knowing that Sam had compassionate friends.

MESSAGES FROM SAM: It wasn't until the week following Sam's passing that I discovered the depth of Sam's love for me. Apparently, throughout her life here, she told countless schoolmates and college friends about me. And they knew about her desire to protect me.

From the other side, Sam often expresses her empathy and understanding of my physical conditions. During one session, she said, "I'm sorry, Mom. I'm sorry it's like that."[1] Her compassion wasn't just a characteristic she had here—it's a major quality of Sam's soul. While I'm still here, she wants me to be as comfortable and as happy as possible.[2]

I asked Sam to recall our excursion to shop for her eighteenth birthday party. She didn't say anything but instead flashed images of a bunch of different costumes, which captured the essence of our fun afternoon there. The store was loaded with costumes.[3]

---

1. JD, August 1, 2019
2. SH, January 30, 2019; JD, September 3, 2020
3. JD, October 5, 2018

A Step Forward

The year before she completed high school, Sam researched colleges that had animation programs. The University of Central Florida, in Orlando, was one of the few she considered attending. I was thrilled when she decided to apply to UCF and was accepted, as it was only a four-hour drive from Tallahassee.

I had great hopes for her future. But before her new life could begin, we needed to make it through her graduation ceremony.

Determined to watch Sam receive her diploma, I figured out a strategy to protect myself from the masses and their scented products. The lengthy ceremony was held at a large indoor arena, so I moved about outside and periodically popped my head inside to check on Sam's place in line. The fragrances were overwhelming, and I struggled with dizziness and lung irritation.

I feel so fortunate, though, to have been able to make it through the discomfort and see my angel graduate. Afterward, my mother, Max, and I were there with hugs and flowers. For me, this special moment was rewarding and joyous. But I remember how uncomfortable Sam looked. I've always wondered what specifically had upset her that night. Maybe she was disappointed that her father hadn't come. I can't recall the reason he gave her for not being there, but he did live several states away.

There were large crowds of family and friends around other students. Perhaps Sam felt underrepresented. Later, my sister said she was there with my niece, but they left before the crowd dispersed, and Sam didn't know they had been there.

MESSAGES FROM SAM: I asked Sam why she looked uncomfortable in the pictures of her high school graduation. Immediately, she responded that she'd hated graduation. She felt anxious about participating in a large public event and said she would rather have been a wallflower fading into the background. Just the thought of being singled out when she received her diploma caused her distress.

She was also disturbed about the uncertainty of what came next in her life. Reflecting on that time in her life, I imagine she worried about going away to college, not knowing anyone there, and how much of a challenge it might be.

Although I had considered Sam a forthcoming teenager, I now know she kept a lot of concerns to herself. I wish I had known more about her worries and fears. How had I missed these things? It wasn't until after she passed that Sam admitted that there were things in her life that she didn't discuss with anybody.[1]

Whenever I get upset about not being in tune with my daughter's emotional needs, I try to focus on the uplifting messages she has given me about the good job I did as a mother.[2] *Her awareness of my love for her has been the most fulfilling to hear. "I always felt loved." She also acknowledged that she always knew I would be there for her when she needed me.*[3]

---

1. SH, October 3, 2016
2. SH, October 3, 2016; JF, September 7, 2016; BH, Early 2018; SH, January 10, 2018; KB, August 8, 2018; JD, August 17, 2018; JD, December 11, 2018
3. JD, December 11, 2018

Heavenly Shoes

Adding to the anxiety of the graduation ceremony, Sam felt physical pain. Her feet hurt in the dressy shoes she wore. I never knew this. It all makes me sad. But on a good note, perhaps she wasn't as disappointed as I had presumed by the lack of family presence at the ceremony.[4]

When she was young, Sam wore a variety of cute shoes without any discomfort. But as she got older, the shape and size of her feet meant that she couldn't enjoy wearing dressy or fun shoes. However, I have discovered that Sam had, and still has, a fascination with shoes.

Since her death, Sam has flashed several images of cute, fun shoes. A few months after her passing, she said she was "around a lot of shoes." This puzzled me.[5] The next shoe reference came exactly two years after her passing. She held up a pair of yellow strappy sandals and adamantly pointed at them.[6] I was still confused.

Another time, she illustrated in perfect detail my favorite sandals. I have only worn them on special occasions. Two of those times were at events that honored Sam. Maybe she thought they were pretty. They were a unique combination of feminine and comfortable, and they could be either casual or dressy.[7]

Then one day, she joked about her fondness for shoes. "Sometimes I go looking at shoes. And buying shoes." And then she brought up the adorable plastic sandals called "jellies" that she wore as a child here. She really liked them. It's possible that was the last time she was able to comfortably wear a fun pair of girlie shoes.

But now she can wear anything. "It doesn't matter what you put on your feet. They feel divine."

---

4. JD, April 25, 2019
5. CL, January 1, 2016
6. SH, July 7, 2017
7. SH, October 2017

Sam finally explained her shoe situation when she was here. She said shoes, in this particular life, either made her feet hurt or were uncomfortable. "Even though I didn't like shoes for myself," she said, "I loved shoes." She admired them on other people. For me, this was another example of a longing she never shared with me. She said it was just one of those insignificant things that you don't really think to share with somebody. She especially loved heels and wild-looking shoes. She admitted that besides being physically uncomfortable, she didn't have the confidence to wear them. Her weight contributed to her insecurity.

My heart swells with joy when I think about the fulfillment Sam now gets from her physical appearance. She no longer has any concerns about size, shape, or discomfort. And she can express her personality by wearing whatever she wants.

To conclude her little chat about shoes, Sam presented one of her legs—now thin—wearing a pair of high heels with ribbons like those on ballet pointe shoes, laced all the way up her leg. She exclaimed, "Whatever you want, you can do!"[8]

---

8. JD, December 21, 2018

On the Road

Max and I decided to sell our house during the middle of Sam's senior year in high school. Unable to be in or around the public, I no longer had a job that helped pay our bills. And since our mortgage was the largest financial drain on us, it needed to be eliminated.

Sam moved into my mother's home while our house was on the market, and Max and I joined her a few weeks later, when it sold. While we began our search for a new location to better meet my health needs, Sam finished her senior year.

Max and I thought South Florida, with its warm coastal air, would be a good place for me. Pete, his friend and former co-owner of the restaurant, had moved to Fort Myers three years prior. He and his partner, Cindy, kindly offered their couches while we checked out the area.

And so, we drove Sam to college in Orlando in the fall of 2009 with plans to stay at Pete's house, until we found our own place. Max and I each drove a car packed with both Sam's belongings and our own travel stuff. (When I travel, we have to bring our own linens, pillows, special food, and a large air purifier, among other necessities. We also pack more clothes than most because we can't use others' washing machines.)

Robert, who had officially become Sam's ex-boyfriend, rode with another friend in a third car, carrying more of

Sam's belongings. Max and I paid for their gas and food and gave them money for their time and effort.

Sam and I rode together in my car. The stressful and tiring drive was only the beginning of a long and emotional day for both of us. I wish I could do this important day all over again.

Sam still loved Robert, but he no longer felt the same. And unfortunately, on that day, Robert was upset about something, and his disposition reflected it. He departed after all of Sam's belongings had been carried into the apartment in Orlando. Sam looked tormented, and I could see the tears in her eyes.

Although the university offered on-campus housing, it didn't offer the kind of privacy Sam preferred. I think low self-image played a big part in her decision. Sam's apartment consisted of four bedrooms, each with its own bathroom. Her three roommates were at least a year older than she was. They had lived in the apartment the previous year and knew each other fairly well. Sam knew none of them, which concerned me—but then, she didn't know anyone at the school.

I wanted to take my time helping Sam set up her bedroom and get settled. This was a once-in-a-lifetime event for me, and I wanted everything to be the best it could be for Sam's new beginning. But first, Max and I made a run to the local grocery store to pick up food and basic cleaning supplies for Sam. Her bathroom needed immediate cleaning. Since she didn't have a car, it might be a couple of days before she figured out a bus schedule or caught any rides with her roomies.

While standing in the checkout line at the store, I longed to be with Sam instead of stuck there. I must have mentioned this to Max because I remember him stressing the importance of dropping off the items and getting on the road as quickly as possible. We had another six or seven hours of driving. I knew this and was already overwhelmed by the thought of it. Because of my health conditions, driving more than an hour was a challenge for me. I wanted to scream. Instead, I just cried inside.

Although Max's point was valid, it didn't change my desire and need to comfort, help, and say goodbye to Sam. I gave into the pressure of the situation but always regretted not saying I needed just a few more minutes. Even if Sam were alive today, I would feel the same. She and I will never get that day back.

Saying goodbye to my Sammy, while her mind and heart were reeling, is a memory I wish I could erase.

MESSAGES FROM SAM: Sam admitted to feeling anxious and nervous the day we took her to college. But she also felt excited. She said she was looking forward to college life but was terrified at the same time. "When I look back, that was one of the days that I realized how much I needed you." She was afraid to leave me, even though she so badly wanted her independence.

Sam acknowledged the tears she cried that day. But she said they were the result of the intensity of everything. The day had been so hectic and chaotic.[1] And I think she knew that as soon as we left, she would be facing a new life all alone.

We spent several weeks in Fort Myers with Pete, Cindy, and their three adorable children. Though being in someone else's environment was difficult in many ways for me, I choose to remember the warmth and tolerance of our hosts.

Max was able to land a manager position at a popular restaurant in the area, so we signed a short-term agreement on a rental house in Cape Coral. We had thought the fragrant chemicals from the house's previous occupants would air out, but they didn't. This sped up our search for a safe home.

I worried a lot about Sam during that first year of college, but I tried not to call her more than once a week. This

---

1. JD, September 3, 2020

led to more meaningful conversations when we did talk. I felt alone and isolated, though.

Max had made friends at work and appeared to be thriving. But I was alone at home, physically unable to work. This was another huge source of guilt for me. I appreciated his dedicated efforts to provide for both of us and was probably more grateful than I expressed. But I was weary from my physical struggles, and I felt unneeded and invisible.

We almost purchased three different homes in the Fort Myers/Cape Coral area. But after a year of looking, we threw in the towel. Other than the warm climate, there were no health benefits for me in South Florida.

Left with no other choice, we returned to my mother's house.

Unexpected Reunion

When we returned to Tallahassee, Max quickly found a job as a cook in a large restaurant in South Georgia and settled into a regular routine. As always, he went with the flow of life and kept his positive disposition. It also helped that he was once again a manageable distance from his children, who lived in North Georgia.

But being back in my hometown became an emotional, as well as physical, challenge for me. I felt a sense of hopelessness and was depressed about not having a permanent, safe place to live after a year of searching in South Florida.

Then Sam made a decision that redirected my focus and lifted my spirits. She had not formed any worthwhile connections at school, and she was homesick for her friends, especially Robert. Although Sam and Robert were no longer in a romantic relationship, the two had maintained a deep friendship and were a major part of each other's support system. Needing a few basic core classes before taking her major requirements, Sam decided to come home for her sophomore year and attend the local junior college.

I felt like a mother again. Sam needed and wanted my help and guidance. I enjoyed helping her find and set up her apartment. Max and I gladly donated some furniture we had in storage to make her new space feel like a home. Sam, two other girls, and Robert split the rent. She got a part-time job at a café within walking distance, and she caught rides to school with Robert.

Sam and I had many phone conversations that year. I was thrilled that she occasionally sought out my input on decisions. She even shared her artwork with me and asked for my advice about selling it. I eagerly jumped at any opportunity to support her.

Was it coincidence that both Sam and I returned home at the same time? I don't think so. I saw much more of her that year than I did any year that followed. I think we both needed to be near each other.

MESSAGES FROM SAM: Since Sam has clearly stated it was in her plan to leave this world when she did, I have wondered if her sophomore year at home was a prearranged gift to the two of us. Recently, I asked her. And she verified, "It wasn't random." But she admitted it wasn't a huge plan. Then she lovingly said, "We got to have that year."[1]

---

1. JD, July 9, 2020

New Cast of Characters

Sam returned to UCF in Orlando for her third year of college. During that year, she upgraded her five-year general animation program to a six-year character animation program. Sam didn't complain about the length of the program, even when she learned that it would take her a total of seven years to finish. There was a prerequisite course that she had to repeat twice, and she'd lost some time staying a full year in Tallahassee. But Sam felt confident about her decision. Her new program would make her much more marketable in her career. As always, I supported her dream.

I worried about Sam adjusting to Orlando, but this time, things started off fairly well. It helped that Robert had decided to attend UCF also. Unfortunately, he started dating Sam's roommate, Emma, and their relationship taunted Sam.

Thankfully, Sam made many new friends and began feeling more at home in Orlando. Being around other artists at school helped. But she really came alive when she found a Pokémon league and discovered a new family. Sam easily made friends with everyone. These were her people. She began going to competitions with the other players and had as much fun traveling with her new friends as she did playing in the competitions.

During Sam's third or fourth year in college, her extra weight began to cause health issues. Realizing she needed medical attention, she went to the university clinic. The staff there recommended she see a specialist. She found an endocrinologist in Orlando who would accept the health insurance that her father provided. He diagnosed her as being prediabetic and prescribed daily medication.

Sam felt good about taking charge in finding her own doctor, and she seemed responsible about taking her medicine. I, on the other hand, felt uncomfortable not knowing much about Sam's condition or her doctor. I got the feeling that Sam didn't want me to interfere. Now in her early twenties and on her own again in Orlando, she wanted to be more independent.

Sometime between her fourth and fifth year at school, Sam acquired a great part-time job at a flower shop. Though she was hired as a temporary driver, her personality and rapport with the customers convinced the owners to offer her a regular position in the store. The two owners, a warm-hearted mother and daughter—as well as the other employees and the resident cats and dog—became yet another family for Sam. I couldn't have asked for more caring people to be there for Sam in my absence.

MESSAGES FROM SAM: Those last few years at school gave Sam the college experience she had hoped for. She said it was "your typical but not typical college experience." It was typical because she had a close-knit group of friends that hung out together and played together. But she felt that the uniqueness of her friends and her made it atypical.

Many of her friends were fellow Pokémon players, but some she knew from school. Her band of buddies frequently gathered at restaurants and occasionally at bars, especially those with food. Sam admitted she wasn't into the sorority and fraternity scene. Her group had their own parties. She described her buddies as eclectic. "People may have thought we were weird or odd because we were just a little different. We liked to do what we liked to do."

Sam said she learned a lot about herself at college and was able to come out of her shell. And it's where her self-confidence flourished. It was during that time that she realized people don't really care what you're doing. They're too busy paying attention to themselves.

To wrap up her comments about college, she declared that overall, she had a good experience and that she enjoyed it.[1]

---

1. JD, November 23, 2020

The Cottage

Since our year in South Florida, Max and I had made three more significant investments in our search for a home in a healthier location—none of which worked out. After spending so much money, time, and energy, we were left with only disappointment. However, staying in Tallahassee kept me close to Sam.

Sensing our frustration in needing our own space, my mother eventually made an offer that we found intriguing: the opportunity to renovate my stepfather's old workshop.

After a lot of deliberation, we decided to demolish the workshop and rebuild a 535-square-foot cottage in its place. In many ways, the situation wasn't ideal. Owning a building on someone else's property was the most obvious concern. We would be without a home if my mother needed to move or left this world before I did. And ever since my mother's generous proposal, some of my siblings have expressed resentment toward me, which has affected me greatly. But despite the conflict, I knew living on my mother's property would the best option for my health.

Max and I took our time coming up with the right plan of action to renovate the workshop. Because of my unique restrictions with building methods and materials, we decided to be our own contractor and hire a consultant. It took over a year to finish the construction of our very small space.

It would bring me great satisfaction to say the cottage

was totally safe for me after its completion. But that wouldn't be the truth. Yes, the cottage had wonderful features that made it a somewhat healthy living space for me. But there were a couple of problems that also made it harmful to me, which unfortunately still exist to this day. These issues were intensified at night, so I slept in a guest bedroom in my mother's house.

To manage these issues during the day, I often open the windows to pull in fresh air. But even when the outside temperature is perfect, there is often woodsmoke or fumes from neighbors' fragranced detergents or lawn maintenance. I usually spend my days in the cottage doing laundry, writing, eating meals, and spending a couple of hours in the evening chatting with Max or watching TV. But sometimes I'm forced to retreat the bedroom in my mother's house, where at least I have a bed and internet.

MESSAGES FROM JACK: To my relief and appreciation, my deceased stepfather, Jack, showed up during my very first session with a medium. Without any prompting from me, he showed images of his workshop being rebuilt and turned into our cottage. And then he expressed his approval.

In that early session, Jack also revealed that he assisted Sam when she first crossed over.[1] Since the rest of her earthly family was still here, it comforted me knowing that Jack was one of the first spirits to greet Sam.

---

1. RL, October 26, 2015

Imaginary Friends

With Sam immersed in her college life in Orlando, emptiness engulfed me. Once again, I found myself envying Max's full life. He made buddies everywhere, even with the employees at the grocery store where he went almost every day. And whenever he could, he traveled to visit his girls in Georgia. Their weekends together gave him something to look forward to.

I, on the other hand, being unable to go out in public without consequences, had unintentionally become a recluse. I knew I needed to find a new interest or hobby to distract me from my self-pity—something creative that didn't require physical repetition or strength.

I pondered what I still enjoyed and could physically do. Three things came to mind: walking, eating, and watching movies. *Okay*, I thought, *but none of these are creative endeavors*. After much thought, though, I realized I was wrong. For months, I'd been thinking there was a huge need for new romantic movies. I had seen all the good ones—both old and new—over and over again. Surely, I could create a story that was as good as some of those produced in the last few years.

Having never done any creative writing, I began reading books on screenwriting. I soon realized that an artistic person might be more successful at writing movies than someone who writes books. Writing a scene description in a screenplay is quite different from writing an eloquent sentence for a novel. Of course, the biggest challenge for any writer is to tell an entertaining story. Needing something fun to focus on, I ignored this point.

Writing a screenplay did indeed give me purpose. And although I had no illusions of it being made into a movie, I unexpectedly discovered something tremendously fulfilling. Through the process of developing characters and their dialogue, I created a world of imaginary friends. I was always thinking about them, and they entertained me far more than characters in someone else's movie.

It took months, but I completed a first draft of the screenplay. A year after that, I finished the revisions.

MESSAGES FROM SAM: Though Sam was still alive when I studied screenwriting, she later suggested that perhaps her death would inspire a screenplay. And although I could write about her, I might also choose to use what I've learned from her to give me an idea for a fictional movie.

She then mentioned that I had an unfinished screenplay.[1] This amazed me. I had started a screenplay a year after Sam's death about a girl Sam's age who had passed unexpectedly and wanted to connect with her mother. It was a romantic drama/comedy. I had stopped working on it around the time I started taking notes for this book. Now, with Sam's encouragement and guidance, I have a renewed motivation to finish it.

---

1. JD, August 6, 2020

Italian Adventure

The last few months of the cottage construction consisted mostly of finishing touches and waiting for the paint to outgas. During this time, Max left his cooking job in Georgia, finally allowing himself the time to reflect on something he might want to pursue outside the restaurant business. He had spent more than twenty-five years as either a restaurant manager or cook working long hours with few days off.

While Max caught his breath, I was dealing with a new health scare. Mammograms were reflecting an alarming development of cysts in my breasts. Both my gynecologist and general surgeon stressed the need for a biopsy. No big deal, right? But with my sensitivities to medicine, including anesthesia, I declined to have the procedure at that time. My gynecologist referred me to an oncologist—I presume to scare me into having the biopsy. I still declined.

I sensed something dreadful was around the corner for me, and I wanted time to be with Max and Sam. I found it very interesting that Max's unemployment situation at that particular time had freed him up to take a trip for as long as he wanted—at least, as long as we could afford it. While working in the restaurant business, he had never been able to take more than a week off at a time.

A dream kept popping up in my mind: Italy. I had studied art in Tuscany one summer while in college, and this life-changing experience had led me to promise Sam that one day I would take her there.

As for Max and me, we had planned to honeymoon in Italy ten years earlier. But because Max had just started his own restaurant a couple of months before our wedding, we decided to postpone the trip and instead spent three days at a beach in West Florida. The honeymoon in Italy never happened.

While Max sorted through his career opportunities, I began to dream of taking Sam to Italy and having my ultimate honeymoon at the same time. I felt the stars aligning; I just knew this was all meant to happen. And I knew we needed to go as soon as possible.

Sharing the Italy dream with Max took a little courage. Fortunately, he heard the immediate need in my voice, and he trusted my intuition—and for this, I'm so grateful.

Max, who is three-quarters Italian, had never been to Italy. Well, not in this lifetime, anyway. His grandparents emigrated from Italy, and his mother has visited multiple times. The family connection alone made the trip enticing for Max. Once I had him hooked, I suggested that we include his oldest daughter, Ashley, who was also in college. We planned to go in early June, when both she and Sam would be on summer break. Sam just needed to get time off from her job at the flower shop.

Although Max wanted his daughter to come with us, he postponed asking her because he felt she wouldn't want to deal with the inconveniences of traveling with me. I understood. But secretly, I believed she would jump at the chance to go to Italy with us, having all her expenses paid. I was right.

But for Ashley and Sam to be able to travel with us, they had to prepare. They began using my fragrance-free products days before the trip. Ashley also gave us all her travel clothes weeks earlier so that we could wash them many times, to remove the fragrances of both her detergent and her apartment. We packed her bag for her, and all she had to do was bring a few essentials in a backpack that we had sent her in the mail. We basically did the same for Sam, except I bought her a few travel clothes that she desperately needed and prewashed them at our house.

I can only assume traveling with me on the plane wasn't fun. And I looked like a weirdo. I wore two masks and several layers of clothing, including a baseball cap. But Sam and Max were extremely kind and supportive every time I had a reaction. Ashley was on a different flight, as she'd started from another location. Lucky her.

We had exceptionally good fortune with our rental car. In the US, I'm unable to ride in other people's cars due to their care products and air fresheners—and never a rental car. Europe is different, though. Some places in Italy do use deodorizers, but I've never encountered air fresheners in the cars there.

I can recall vividly the five-hour drive through the countryside from the Milan airport to our first lodging destination, in the southwest corner of Tuscany. The patchwork of farms, lush vineyards, and peaceful fields that covered the rolling hills elicited emotions that had been hiding deep within my being. I had forgotten the beauty and serenity of the Tuscan landscape. Max and I both teared up several times just taking in the scenery, feeling grateful that we were able to share this incredible experience with Sam and Ashley.

MESSAGES FROM SAM: Sam and I have discussed Italy multiple times since her departure. And once, she acknowledged that I felt like crying whenever I saw images of Italy. This moved me deeply. She explained that I have a longing for it, that it feels like home, and it's my soul's favorite place. And she repeated this a year and a half later.[1] All of this was, and is, absolutely true!

---

1. JD, May 9, 2019; JB, November 9, 2020

Twice, Sam has told me about a "sweet life" Max and I had had in Italy. We were romantic partners but not married. Max was the male, as he was in most of our other lives together. Max's soul doesn't like being a female. It makes him feel too weak, too vulnerable.[2] Even though my family in that life didn't approve of our union, we were happy. We lived off the land, away from others. Sam said the isolation was an important part of that life. "It was very peaceful."[3]

We had divided the trip into two lodgings of eight nights each. In preparation, I had searched extensively for chemical-free rentals and discovered that organic farms offered the healthiest accommodations for me. I succeeded in finding an organic farm for the first half of the trip. Located in an area called the Maremma, it was a rustic apartment that suited us perfectly.

It didn't take us long to get into the swing of Italian life. We would visit the local butcher and grocery store almost daily and prepare delicious meals every night. Max did all the cooking but enlisted assistance with some of the prep work. I can still remember our first meal at the farm. Sam and Ashley sat outside snapping the ends of fresh green beans while the sun was setting over the rolling hills. It had been several years since Sam and Ashley had spent time together. Now, they were able to catch up.

On days when we traveled, I'd pack a yummy sandwich made from the leftovers of dinner the night before, tons of cheese, and Italian bread. Oh, how I love Italian bread. It has no preservatives. We bought it fresh daily, just like the Italians. The others bought lunch from vendors and cafes. We took excursions almost every day of our trip. Although we wanted to hit the major tourist destinations, we invited suggestions from the owner of the farm. We visited Rome

---

2. JD, March 29, 2019
3. JD, September 7, 2018

twice and Pisa while staying in this area. They both exceeded our expectations. And two of the recommended not-so-famous destinations, Saturnia and Porto Ercole, became our favorites of the entire trip.

My heart aches when I relive our day in Saturnia. I associate both good and bad moments with this small town's major attraction—its thermal springs. The water of Saturnia's biggest spring comes out of the ground and flows down a small stream that cascades over rocks and creates little waterfalls that form aqua-colored pools where locals and tourists lounge and play.

When we first arrived at this spring, Sam slipped on a large, wet rock, skinning her knee and twisting her ankle. I saw how she fell: her ankle was bent awkwardly underneath her. But to my astonishment, her ankle wasn't seriously injured or a major source of pain. Her skinned knee, however, caused a lot of discomfort for several nights and days.

Sam and I soaked in one of the smaller pools of the hot spring while Max and Ashley sat nearby in another pool. I can't recall discussing anything important as we sat together in that warm, shallow pool surrounded by gorgeous scenery,

but I have clung to the memory countless times since. We shared a unique and thoroughly enjoyable experience. And I'm certain that the sulfur water gave Sam's leg a jump-start on healing.

> *MESSAGES FROM SAM: I asked Sam what she recalled from our day at the thermal springs in Saturnia. Her immediate response made me laugh: "The smell." But she then admitted that she didn't mind the sulfur odor like I did.*
>
> *Sam's next comment made a bigger impact on me. She acknowledged the time we spent alone and stressed the "closeness" that she and I experienced there. This really struck a chord with me. To comfort myself during the first couple of years following Sam's passing, I would frequently visualize the two of us sitting in the warm pool of water in Saturnia, as we enjoyed the beautiful landscape that surrounded us. Wow! She confirmed that it had been something special for her also.*
>
> *When I asked Sam about hurting her leg at the thermal springs, she showed an image of herself falling and the abnormal position of her leg. She said divine intervention had prevented a serious injury.*[4]

Remarkably, Sam rarely said anything about her leg pain. I could read her face, though. As the four of us traveled through the towns, Sam's pace slowed. She would overheat and quickly tire from exertion.

Whenever Sam needed to rest, Max and Ashley often went ahead. On top of the oozing, scraped-up knee that hurt when she walked, Sam was overweight and out of shape. I felt for her. Although I was happy that Max and Ashley were together and able to see as much as time allowed, Sam felt rejected, time and time again.

---

4. JD, August 6, 2020

By the second half of the trip, Sam's leg was on the mend. However, she still couldn't keep up. When I stopped to keep her company, more often than not I, too, needed to catch my breath. Walking the hilltop towns of Italy can be exhausting for anybody.

For our final eight days, we stayed at an attractive renovated villa east of Siena, in Central Tuscany. It was pesticide-free and about as fragrance-free as the organic farm. And the villa worked out almost as well as the farm. We found two grocery stores nearby with fresh food. Our charming and rustic apartment at the villa had a well-equipped, modern kitchen. And just as on the first half of the trip, we managed to see the big attractions, as well as those suggested by the villa's owner. Among the well-known cities we visited were Siena, Florence, and Cortona, where I had studied art thirty-five years earlier.

Despite the hurt and humiliation Sam felt because of her slow pace, this trip was one of the most wonderful I've ever experienced. Sharing Italy with Sam meant so much to me. And it was the adventure of a lifetime!

MESSAGES FROM SAM: Sam admitted that her weight was the biggest reason for the difficulty in keeping up with everyone. She felt short of breath and overheated during our excursions. Interestingly, Sam takes full credit for her physical condition. "Mom, I created that situation. That was one of my struggles and challenges." Her statements reassured me that I couldn't have done anything to avoid her weight issue. It was planned before this life.

Good News

Having survived the plane travel and accommodations in Italy, I felt hopeful about the future. I entertained the idea of traveling with Sam again before she settled down with a demanding job or a family.

Hope is a wonderful thing. It gave me the strength to reexamine the issue of the cysts in my breasts. I had another mammogram and ultrasound and braced myself for the results.

The surgeon delivered the news: he saw no change in my breasts, and if this continued, nothing needed to be done. The following screenings, at intervals throughout the next couple of years, confirmed that the cysts had stopped multiplying and everything looked benign.

I wondered if it had all been a ploy to get us to Italy. Regardless, the trip had given me that special time I needed, and wanted, to spend with Sam.

MESSAGES FROM SAM: When I asked Sam about the purpose of our trip to Italy, she confirmed that it was meant to happen. It, too, had been preplanned. Because my subconscious knew she and I would be separating soon, I had felt the urgency to take the trip as soon as possible. My soul had included this trip in our plan to give us those last enjoyable and memorable experiences together.[1] *The*

---
1. JD, September 3, 2020; JB, November 9, 2020

previous five years of her life here had been filled with work and college.

Portrait of an Artist

Throughout her years in college, Sam earned extra money from commissioned artwork. Through an online community of digital artists, she discovered a unique avenue of income. People would pay her to illustrate a scene with their own personal animal characters, which they had created as alternate personalities. Unfortunately, this type of work often interfered with Sam's schoolwork, on top of her job at the flower shop and her Pokémon tournaments.

Even though I expressed concern over Sam's commission load, I was thoroughly impressed with her ability to create this type of art and her unwavering confidence. Although I could still draw at that time, I didn't have the ability to illustrate like she could, and I certainly couldn't have handled that kind of creative pressure.

Through the digital artist community, Sam made wonderful friends that became yet another family away from home. She felt so close to some that she would travel long distances to meet up with them. She also registered as an artist at conventions and produced on-the-spot commissions for the attendees.

I distinctly recall the phone conversation Sam and I had after she attended the senior film presentation of her roommate, Emma, who was a year ahead of Sam in the animation program. Known as "Final Films," the presentation showcased two short animated films created by the graduating class. The experience ignited Sam's motivation to finish the animation program.

She called me soon after to express how much she wanted me to share this exciting moment with her the following year. She went so far as to say, "Mom, if you have to choose between watching me graduate and the Final Films, please come to the films." Knowing what a challenge it would be for me to attend a public event, she said I could stand in the back, far from the fragrances and chemicals of others. And then she shared her wishes to be standing right there next to me. Overwhelmed by the thought that she wanted me, above everyone else, to be with her, I started to cry. I assured her that I wouldn't miss it for the world.

MESSAGES FROM SAM: Sam left us a few weeks after that emotional phone call, with one year to go in her animation program. About a year and a half later, out of the blue, she apologized to me for not finishing college. But then she said it wasn't really an apology. Even though the time of her death had been planned, she expressed that I might have felt let down by not seeing her graduate.

Of course, I would have thoroughly enjoyed standing next to her, beaming with pride and crying, as we watched the Final Films together. But in no way did her not completing college cause me sadness or distress. Sam probably would have worked herself too hard, as it was going to be an intensive year in her program. And we both would likely have been frustrated with the brief one or two visits she might have managed to squeeze in.[1]

---

1. SH, November 23, 2016

Part II

A New Beginning

~~~~~

It was the Fourth of July, 2015. This year the holiday fell on a Saturday. Max and I listened to a neighbor's fireworks while watching fireworks on TV. The evening started out pleasant, until the air quality diminished. It was too hot outside to open the windows and air out the cottage. A year had passed since its completion, and I still couldn't sleep there. But that night, I finally bit the bullet and attempted to stay. I went to bed with my head covered by a couple of sheets to protect my nose, throat, and lungs. It was a long and uncomfortable night, and I awoke around six thirty with a heavy heart.

The sun was coming up and the makings of a beautiful new day were present. No matter how difficult my nights were, I always tried to find hope in waking to a sunny morning. But on this day, sadness overcame me. I felt as if I would never really be comfortable sleeping in our cottage. Max was still sleeping, and I didn't want to disturb him. I covered my face with my sheets again and dozed off.

This weekend, Sam was in Indianapolis, Indiana, participating in the Pokémon US National Championship. She and a group of fellow players had driven from Orlando, taking shifts at the wheel. Sam had told me she'd planned on driving through the night and had prepared herself by changing her sleeping habits the previous week. As a mother who constantly worried about her daughter's health, I didn't like this.

Three days before, I had spoken with Sam as she took off with her pals. We always talked on the phone when she began a trip, as well as when she arrived at her destination. She left me a brief message the following day to let me know she'd arrived at the tournament center and had made it to their hotel room to get settled in. I presume Sam took a nap then. Or at least, I hoped she did.

Thinking about her all day on Friday and Saturday, I had to restrain myself from calling and checking on her. I knew that she was busy having fun. She thoroughly enjoyed these competitions and had done very well at the national tournament the previous year. Even if Sam wasn't winning, she'd be having a blast. I looked forward to hearing about everything on Sunday, after the last round of the tournament. If no one in her carpool had done well, they might leave early Sunday morning. But chances were, they would want to hang around to see their fellow Orlando Pokémon-mates play.

At around seven Sunday morning, my phone rang. Either something good had happened at the tournament or no one in Sam's group had made it to the final round and they were too disappointed to stay and watch.

As always, I answered the call in a tone that was as upbeat as possible, hiding anything that might be troubling me. I probably offered one of my usual greetings like "Well, hello, sweetheart!" or "Good morning, pumpkin!" I can't remember my exact words. But everything that followed is permanently etched into my mind.

Sam didn't respond. After a pause, someone spoke. "Beverly, this is Avery. I'm calling because I know how close you and Sam are."

My head started to spin. *Why is Sam's best friend calling me? And what does she mean? Of course we're close. What's going on?*

Avery proceeded to explain that something was wrong with Sam and EMTs were on their way. Sam's hotel roommates had found her on the floor in the bathroom, unconscious. I knew from her tone that it was bad. Really bad. I asked Avery to call me as soon as the EMTs got there. Then I quickly told Max what I knew and asked him to answer my phone and to look for the soonest flight to Indianapolis. Shaking, I ran into my mother's house to quickly dress and pack.

I was in the bathroom, frantically gathering my things, when Max lightly tapped on the door and slowly opened it. I could see the disbelief and pain in his eyes. Not wanting to delay the inevitable, he quickly but gently told me Sam was gone.

I collapsed in his arms, wailing. I don't recall how long he held me, but eventually he took me to my mother's living room and sat down next to me. In his arms, I continued to scream and cry.

What happened during the next few hours surprised me. I instinctively knew to keep moving, to do my mundane, everyday chores. In retrospect, I believe I intuitively knew that I would shut down for a very long time if I didn't keep moving.

Max offered to call David to deliver the news. Still in shock, I accepted his offer. I could barely communicate, and I expected David would want answers. Unfortunately, at that point, there was no conclusive cause of death.

Within an hour or two, I received a phone call from the coroner's office. I needed to identify the body. Images of my precious daughter's dead body were sent via email. It was excruciating to see her lifeless face on my screen. To make this horrific moment even worse, in the picture, foam surrounded her mouth. I wondered why no one had had the sense to clean her face before taking the image to send to me. Perhaps procedure prevented any alterations to a body before the autopsy.

Throughout the day, the same thoughts circled in my mind: *My angel is gone, and I didn't even get to hold her. What happened and how long did she suffer? Being alone, she must have been frightened. How long will I survive life without her?*

Soon after responding to the coroner's email, David called to express his disapproval that I had already identified the body. Apparently, he thought I was being disrespectful by not asking him to participate in this horrifying task. Already devastated, I could barely function. And now I had to deal with David's anger.

As the day progressed, I began to feel a sense of relief that Sam no longer lived among us. As a mother, I had constantly worried about how much her heavy body and other physical issues burdened her. She frequently faced rejection because of her appearance. And for years, she had agonized over concealing her romantic and sexual preferences. Sam was attracted to people regardless of gender or race, and she lived in fear of her father's disapproval of these preferences. And yet, she desperately wanted her dad to know her and accept her.

Fortunately, Sam had just seen David before her passing. She had called me following a weeklong visit with his family and reported what a healing experience it had been. Her father had finally accepted her for who she was and expressed his unconditional love. I shared in her joy.

MESSAGES FROM SAM: That last visit with her dad had been prearranged. Sam said it was in her soul's plan to have this experience before she passed. She explained that the confidence that had been building the past few years at college had helped her to disclose her bisexuality to her dad.

Sam emphasized the importance of the healing that took place. And although it was more for David, because he was still living, it benefited her soul also. "Had that not happened," she said, "we would have carried energy that we would have had to deal with over here or in the next life together."[1]

---

1. JD, November 23, 2020

When I reflect on those few weeks before Sam departed, I can see how hopeful she was about her future. In addition to her motivation to complete her animation program, she was excited about a new relationship. Since Robert, Sam hadn't felt strongly about anyone romantically. This relationship was with a female—a fellow artist named Sophie. I believe this romance led Sam to open up to her father during their last visit together.

It seems odd that I would feel relief about Sam's departure from this world when her earthly future finally looked promising. But my beliefs about heaven prompted this emotion. I was taught that heaven is the ultimate place of love and acceptance. And so, I believed—no, I knew—the joy in Sam's afterlife would far exceed any happiness she found here.

Now that I had accepted Sam's departure as a blessing, I had to face the nightmare of living without her. I didn't know how to do this. All I could think to do was to remind myself that Sam was free of struggles and surrounded by love.

It had been five months since I'd seen her, which now seemed so unfair. I had encouraged her not to come home for Mother's Day because she had a lot of schoolwork and other commitments to handle. Instead, she sent me a heartwarming card that captured the true essence of our relationship. It was one of those cards that I would have cherished for a lifetime even if she had lived to send me a hundred more.

The day that Sam died seemed endless. As that long day turned into a sleepless night, I spoke to Sam between episodes of crying. I asked her why her spirit hadn't come to see me after she left. I had heard stories of other people's loved ones visiting them—usually in a dream—the moment they departed. Had our special bond not warranted that?

MESSAGES FROM SAM: Sam explained that because her death was unexpected, she was busy assimilating after departing.[2]

Some parents might have lost their minds waiting to hear how their child died. I did not, even though it took two months for the coroner's office to provide a cause of death. I think this had a lot to do with Sam's age. When young adults are unexpectedly found dead, overdose is often a suspected cause. This unfortunate preconception wasted a lot of time. The final cause of death was acute pancreatitis.

MESSAGES FROM SAM: One of the interesting aspects of my early conversations with Sam after her passing was her lack of desire to talk about what had happened. Many mediums like to address the cause of death, mostly because it provides validation for the client. In Sam's case, though, she felt it was irrelevant. She doesn't like providing information that she knows I don't need to hear over and over again.

Several times, she has expressed her displeasure with inquiries about her death. Four years after her passing, when a new medium pried about it, Sam expressed her frustration with a hand gesture, brushing away the subject. And then she said, "We've been through this."[3]

However, every once in a while, she reluctantly offers information about her death. The following are the bits and pieces she has divulged:

- *Her death was nobody's fault.*[4]
- *She didn't die at home.*[5]
- *She felt sick, so she went to the bathroom. "I thought I ate something bad or something that didn't agree with me. I didn't know I was going to die." She felt toxic, disoriented,*

---

2. BH, Early 2018
3. SH, November 23, 2016; MG, November 1, 2019
4. BH, Early 2018
5. BH, April 27, 2017

*and confused.*⁶ *During another session with a different medium, Sam used almost the same wording: "I didn't think I was going. I thought maybe I was sick. But I didn't think I was that sick." And then she showed an image of the bathroom where she died.*⁷

- *She passed quickly and unexpectedly.*⁸ *There was a "jolt" in her head and then "lights out." She didn't suffer long. Sam assured me, "It didn't hurt much."*⁹

- *There was nothing anyone could have done to save her.*¹⁰

Of course, knowing why and how Sam died wasn't going to bring her back. And I already knew that Sam didn't cause her own death, not knowingly anyway. She just got sick. In the past, she had told me how sick she would get from eating or drinking the wrong things.

Her suffering was my only concern. The images of her last hours swirled through my thoughts and haunted me.

*MESSAGES FROM SAM: To comfort me, Sam assured me that she was greeted upon her arrival to the other side. "I wasn't alone. I wasn't scared." During three different conversations, she stressed it was important that I know this.*¹¹

*She has reinforced the message that her life was meant to end at the time it did.*¹² *Three times, Sam has told me that there was nothing she or I could have done to make the end of her life turn out differently.*¹³

Sam also expressed that she was satisfied with her life here, even though she had many struggles. "I wouldn't change a thing." She is happy with all of her life's experiences

---

6. JD, July 18, 2018
7. BH, Early 2018
8. BH, April 27, 2017; JD, July 18, 2018
9. JF, September 7, 2016; BH, April 27, 2017; BH, Early 2018
10. BH, April 27, 2017
11. JF, September 7, 2016; BH, April 27, 2017; JD, July 18, 2018
12. VD, March 15, 2019; JD, March 18, 2019
13. SH, November 23, 2016; BH, April 27, 2017; JD, July 18, 2018

and challenges. She has no regrets whatsoever.[14] *She later explained why: if we lived a life in which we learned the lessons we had planned, it's considered a huge accomplishment.*[15]

Many times, I have expressed to Sam my sadness over not being with her when she died. Not being able to comfort her. Not being able to hold her one last time. But she has informed me that it was preplanned for her to be alone when she departed. The last time I told her that I wished I could have been there, she responded, "No, Mom. You don't." And as she often does, she then lightened the mood. "No. Mommy Salami, I would not have wanted you to be there."[16] That's my Sammy!

Homecoming

It wasn't until later that I learned what actually happened when Sam crossed over. Immediately upon her death, a guide took Sam from her body. She said it happened quickly and, at that moment, she was aware of only one guide. It was dark. Then she saw light and instantly found herself in it. "I go from dark to light. And then I can see that there are so many others." *They had been there all along. She just couldn't see them when she was alive.*

No one was communicating with her yet because she needed to get oriented. She found herself walking in a field.[17] "When I first got there, I was walking in wildflowers." *Barefoot, she walked for a few yards to get "grounded." She said,* "I knew I had died." *However, she acknowledged that she needed the short walk through the flowers "to process." Not surprisingly, spirits can process things much quicker over*

---

14. GK, November 16, 2015; JF, September 7, 2016; SH, April 11, 2017; SH, October 2017
15. JD, April 13, 2020
16. JD, July 2, 2020
17. JD, September 3, 2020

there. *"Your brain can process so fast here."*[18]

After her brief walk, others greeted her. *"Then it all started. And I was right in the middle of it."* There was a lot of activity, with a lot of spirits. Sam teased, *"It's like Santa's workshop on Christmas Eve."*[19] Even though it was hectic, she had the ability to understand and hear everybody.[20]

Sam later explained what happens at most arrivals. *"When you get over here, you see the family that you knew when you were in that life [who had already passed]. But they're not always the ones that you were closest with."* She said there are *"all these other ones, too, who are part of your soul family, that weren't with you this lifetime."* She summed up the sensation of being welcomed home: *"The amount of love is not even comparable to anything we can feel on earth."*

Because her life here was short, it didn't take Sam long to get reacclimated to the other side. To her, it seemed to happen quickly. However, time is very different over there. She said if we think of it in terms of our time here, *"It was a couple of weeks later that I started to do my life review."*[21]

Sam clarified that spirits have different homecoming experiences when they return to heaven, depending on their personality or needs. Her celebration began immediately, with souls cheering: *"You're home! You're back!"* Understanding Sam's relief over leaving all the challenges and trauma of a human life, others rejoiced with her.

In attempting to describe her emotions about being home, Sam gave an entertaining analogy. She said a human life is like taking a trip to someplace very far from the US, like Australia, and having a horrible time. And then you travel all the way back home. When you get home,

---

18. JD, November 9, 2018
19. JD, November 9, 2018
20. JD, October 29, 2019
21. JD, November 9, 2018

you are so relieved and grateful to be there that none of the disasters that happened on the trip matter anymore. "You're just so glad to be home."[22]

---

22. JD, October 29, 2019

Misplaced Emotions

The week following Sam's death was the worst week of my life. Thankfully, organizing a funeral service for friends and family proved to be a useful distraction. Looking back, it's obvious that my mind was not exactly clear, and I made a couple of not-so-good decisions.

Getting enough food and sleep became a challenge. At bedtime, my mind continued to torment me with thoughts of Sam's last hours alive. My heart ached for her. And my body couldn't relax. Unable to get restful sleep, I would finally give up the fight when I saw daylight. I had no desire to eat. Trust me when I say that, under ordinary circumstances, this is unusual for me. I enjoy food. But I did drink enough water to stay hydrated, and I forced myself to eat a little food whenever I felt my blood sugar drop.

During those first two days of unbearable pain, I had to speak with David. When we finally connected over the phone, we discussed cremating Sam. Both of us seemed okay with this decision. David chose to drive to Indianapolis, in hopes of seeing the body and to locate the best place to handle the cremation, which would take at least two days.

In the past, I had anguished over the news of other people losing a child. I imagined the parents would never recover and that their lives would forever be ruined by the oppressive emptiness. So, when I lost my only child unexpectedly, the callous behavior of certain people confused me. As a matter of fact, it crushed me. David's actions during that week were the most hurtful. Apparently, I had once again disrespected him.

I presume he was upset about the fact that during our call, I had asked if he was planning to attend the service. To me, it seemed like a reasonable question. He lived several states away and I wasn't sure his family could physically make the trip. A family member had a health condition that I believed made travel difficult or maybe even impossible. It had crossed my mind that David might prefer to hold a separate service in his town.

David was so hurt that I hadn't assumed he'd be attending the funeral of his daughter that he decided to send me a long email expressing his disapproval. The message appeared to criticize me for anything and everything he believed I had done wrong since Sam's passing—and throughout the years of her life since the divorce. As I started to read the email, I cried in disbelief. Tears rolled so hard and fast that I couldn't even finish it. I never did.

To this day, I still cannot understand how anyone could be so hurtful to another grieving parent. I was just trying to stay above water. Perhaps the unbearable loss of our daughter had triggered emotions that needed an outlet—and blaming me was the release that helped him at that time.

MESSAGES FROM SAM: When I reflect on David's hurtful words now, I try to feel compassion for him. "It's a lot easier to be nice and compassionate over here than it is there," Sam admitted, with a touch of playfulness.[1]

What has helped me move past any hurt I might have unknowingly caused David are Sam's statements about me as her mother. "You were a good mom to me." Several times, she has acknowledged that I not only believed in her, but that I was a loving mother who took good care of

---

1. JD, December 31, 2019

her and watched out for her.[2]

Those comforting words have carried me through many rough times. When I ponder the reason why I was born, I feel fulfilled knowing that one of my life's purposes was bringing this beautiful spirit into this world and having the opportunity to nurture her while she was here. Her life was a gift to me. And although some might believe her life was taken from me, I see it differently. She has never left me. Even though I can't see, hear, or feel her, I know she's here watching over me, listening to everything I say to her, and trying to guide and comfort me. And even laughing at me sometimes. Probably a lot.

---

2. JF, September 7, 2016; SH, October 3, 2016; JD, April 13, 2020

Bobby Pins

That first week after Sam left, I drove to my favorite empty parking lot and walked every day in an attempt to deal with the overwhelming pain and stress. While I walked, I chatted with Sam. I prayed, too. Whether it was God, angels, or other divine beings, I knew someone was holding me up. A lot more than usual. I felt calmer and stronger after every walk.

One morning, in the middle of that surreal week, something extraordinary happened. To describe the event accurately, I need to go back to seven or eight months before Sam's passing. Around that time, I had dropped a large bobby pin while rearranging my hair during my daily walk. I knew exactly where the pin had fallen, yet when I looked down it wasn't there. I became annoyed, as my hair kept falling down without that last pin.

I'll admit, a black bobby pin could have been somewhat camouflaged on a faded asphalt parking lot. But I knew about where it landed, so it shouldn't have been that difficult to find. Every time I passed the spot where I thought it should be, I would look for it. I finally stopped searching after a few weeks. Apparently, the bobby pin had vanished.

Fast-forward to my walk a couple of days after Sammy's departure. I felt a bobby pin coming loose. So as not to lose another pin, I stopped and stood very still while rearranging my hair. But I dropped one anyway. When I looked down to retrieve it, it wasn't there.

Really?! I felt as if I were going crazy. Of all the times for my mind to be tested. I started screaming and crying. This insignificant loss had set off a release of grief and pain that I had attempted to keep at bay. I looked to the heavens and asked why this was necessary. "I know I can't have Sam back, but can I at least have my pin back?" The emotional explosion didn't last long, and I decided to keep moving, as I had been doing ever since hearing of Sam's death. As I had been doing my whole life.

I continued along my routine path in the parking lot. When I reached the spot where I had lost my first bobby pin, something caught my eye. I looked down, and there before my feet lay my pin from months ago. *Whoa! That's really strange*, I thought. *Is this a message? And if so, what is it?*

Completing another loop of my walk, I passed by the location of that day's pin disappearance. In plain sight, the bobby pin was exactly where I had dropped it. I started to cry again. I knew Sam was there. And the message was, *Yes, we have been holding you up.*

MESSAGES FROM SAM: *Sam confessed to me that she'd enlisted the help of a guide to carry out this little magic trick, to get my attention. Some spirits have the ability to move objects here on earth. Sam does not (though she can move a piece of paper with a slight breeze).* She said, *"I couldn't do that. I had to get one of your guides to do it—to get your attention."* She added, *"I had to."* Before I revealed to the medium that the bobby pins had been recovered, Sam told her, *"She got both of them."*[1]

To my delight, this wasn't the only time Sam would employ help from others in physically moving something to send me a message or cheer me up. Although she can't move most objects, she does have the ability to interfere with

---
1. JD, September 21, 2018

electrical or battery-operated appliances and devices, including computers.[2] In one instance, when I was researching distressing information, Sam opened Pandora on my computer and played one of my favorite songs to let me know it was time to stop. Later, she said I was going down a rabbit hole and it was draining my energy. "You were opening Pandora's box." Proud of her play on words, she added, "Isn't that clever?"[3]

Years later, I asked Sam what she felt when she saw the pain I experienced from losing her. "Over here, we don't feel sad for you. We don't feel sorry for you. What I felt for you was immense love." She explained spirits feel empathy for us because they know how tough it is to live a human life. And that's why they spend so much time around us, hoping we'll feel their love.[4]

During another conversation, Sam shared something similar. I was inquiring about whether spirits hurt when they see their loved ones hurting here. "No," she said, "because we don't have that hurt over here." She said spirits understand why we need to suffer—it gives us the opportunity to learn what we wanted to learn. "For me, I'm happy that you are able to grow your soul, because when you do come home, you're going to be happy you had this experience."[5]

---

2. JD, December 21, 2018; JD, January 8, 2019; JD, April 25, 2019; JD, May 9, 2019; JD, June 15, 2019; JD, February 6, 2020; JD, July 2, 2020
3. JD, January 8, 2019
4. JD, July 2, 2019
5. JD, October 5, 2018; JD, June 15, 2019

Tarnished by Lipstick

I haven't been to many funerals, so I don't have much to go on, but Sam's service was the worst I've ever experienced, and not just because it was for my daughter. It was held at the Episcopal church that both Sam and I had attended during our childhood years. We stopped going around the time I could no longer tolerate fragrances. Thankfully, in high school, Sam found a youth group associated with a non-denominational church. I felt relieved that my health hadn't kept her from being part of a spiritual community.

Unfortunately, I didn't know the current rector, but my mother, who still attended services and enjoyed weekly study groups there, strongly discouraged me from having the service at another parish. I heeded her wishes. This was a mistake—one of a few I made that week. My desire not to offend my mother's minister won out over having a service that met my needs.

Distraught and weary, I met with the rector a couple of days before the service. He went through the church's funeral liturgy and asked me to choose the options I preferred. The basic service did not inspire me, and neither did the choices of passages. But that wasn't the worst part. He said that he would speak about Sam unless there was someone else who wanted that honor. I certainly didn't want to speak. Not only would I become too emotional, I have a huge fear of public speaking. Since the rector had never met

Sam, I asked him what he would say. His response horrified me. "Oh, I'll just wing it." *Was he kidding?* Apparently not.

Here I am, barely able to discuss the service of my dead daughter, and he's casually telling me he'll make up stuff on the spot. I wanted to scream at him. Had I not been so unstable at that time, I would have spoken up immediately.

Disturbed beyond belief, I dwelled on this for a whole day. Then I contacted David and asked if he wanted to speak at the service. He said he would do it. Relieved, I then called the church office and asked to speak with the minister. The receptionist said he was unavailable and that she would give him a message. I clearly stated I did not want him to speak about Sam at her service and that her father would do it. I emphasized that it was important he receive this message. I should have called back until I finally reached him. Another huge mistake.

On July 11, 2015, a warm, sunny Saturday, the service took place just outside the church. Although there was a large cemetery next to the property, a small garden had been created for parishioners who preferred cremation. Inside the church was a plaque inscribed with the names of those buried in the garden. The ashes were all mixed up in the garden, but I didn't mind. Before the service, I had placed a couple of handfuls of ashes in a bag for myself.

A large crowd of friends, family, and classmates came to celebrate Sam that day. Almost everyone wore casual and colorful clothing, as had been suggested in the obituary. Sam would have wanted it that way. The obituary also included a request for no fragrances or sunscreen—an odd request but a necessary one if I was to be at the service.

As the minister delivered the traditional Episcopal funeral service, I tried to hold on to reality. I can't recall much now, except my thoughts when the minister began speaking about Sam. *What? What is he doing? Did he not get the message?* He started talking about Sam putting on her lipstick and being a party girl out on the town with her friends. *What!* Not only was this man "winging it," he knew nothing about my daughter!

Yes, Sam liked to have fun with her friends. This is something that comforted me and brought me joy. But Sam spent a lot of her life working on her artwork, keeping up with schoolwork, and making extra money to do her preferred fun activities, like playing in Pokémon tournaments. Sam was not a lipstick kind of girl. Maybe on special occasions she applied some makeup, but this was not the Sam friends and family knew.

Following the burial of Sam's ashes, the minister wrapped up the service by inviting everyone to the reception in the building next to the church.

I spoke up. "I believe David would like to say a few words."

The minister replied that it might be better if David waited until we got to the reception hall because everyone was getting hot. David nodded that he liked that idea. It was fine by me, as the harm had already been done.

MESSAGES FROM SAM: Sam validated being both "cremated and buried."[1] She expressed her gratitude for the cremation and jokingly admitted she would have been "creeped out" if her body were in a coffin in the ground.[2]

When I asked Sam if she had any comments about her funeral, she said the service was serious and didn't fit who we were. She confirmed the religious nature of it and that the man who spoke didn't know her.

I gasped when I heard this. She said, "That wasn't me. It's okay. I'm not upset about this." I asked if she knew how much it upset me. She did. But she added that many people present were aware that the minister had said things about her that didn't make sense.[3]

---

1. BH, Early 2018; KB, August 8, 2018
2. BH, Early 2018
3. JD, December 21, 2018

Cake and Balloons

Thankfully, the reception was everything I had hoped it would be. Max had agreed to prepare most of the food for the reception, so I wouldn't have a reaction. (My sensitivities had progressed to the point that I would react to breathing foods, not just eating them.) I coordinated his menu with that of the church group, who volunteered their time to set up the room and prepare some of the food and beverages. A woman I knew from high school acted as the church's liaison for the event. She was a godsend. Genuinely kind, Kim answered my constant questions and kept me calm.

Interestingly, one week before Sam died, I was forced to get a smartphone. Max needed one for work and because we were on a joint plan, apparently I had to get one, too. Today, I wonder if this was more than a coincidence because Kim and many of Sam's friends sent me dozens of text messages offering assistance and support.

I was overwhelmed by the generosity of the people who loved Sam. Avery—Sam's closest girlfriend in Orlando, the one who had handled the issues of Sam's death in Indianapolis—had set up a GoFundMe account to pay for all the funeral expenses. The total amount donated ended up paying for everything, including David's extended family's travel.

MESSAGES FROM SAM: A year after her passing, Sam asked me to thank Avery for helping me with the celebration. Not only had Avery set up the fund that covered all the funeral costs, but with the assistance of a few others, she'd spread the word about the service. "Mom, they helped get people together for you."[1]

Because of my sensitivities to flowers, we had requested no floral arrangements. But a woman at the church arranged a beautiful, non-fragrant floral centerpiece to be placed on the food table. We decorated the tables with balloons and pictures of Sam. It definitely looked like a celebration. It had to be—Sam's life was a gift to all those who really knew her.

When the outdoor service ended, everyone slowly moved to the reception hall, with Max, my family, and me trailing behind. Relief came over me when I entered the room and realized that almost everyone had respected the request of no fragrances. This made it possible for me to go without a mask for most of the event.

The room was filled with cheery reminiscing, and I felt grateful for the outpouring of love that everyone expressed that day. I didn't recognize a few friends of my parents and several of Sam's peers from high school and college, but otherwise I knew almost everyone. Having become a recluse during the past few years, it was odd to see so many people I hadn't seen in a while. I reconnected with a few of my childhood buddies, and we laughed about our past, as well as our current lives. That meant so much to me.

Sam's animation professor came from Orlando with a large group of classmates. She pulled me aside to offer compliments about Sam's talent. This touched me. And many of Sam's Orlando Pokémon buddies drove up as well. Max and one of Sam's childhood friends took photos of all those who came to celebrate with us and say farewell. The pictures are now permanently printed in a memorial book.

---

1. JF, September 7, 2016

I had brought my own food from home. Twice, I managed to sneak away for a couple of minutes to grab a bite in a kitchen closet, where I had left my backpack earlier. I still wasn't eating much, but that was about to change. Earlier in the week, I had ordered a large cake for the reception, from a cake shop in town that both Sam and I adored. The thought of diving into the cake after the gathering had become increasingly attractive over the past couple of days. I instinctively knew that I would be calmer when everything was over. And I knew I would actually want to eat cake then—possibly a lot of cake.

In the middle of the reception, David asked his oldest son to join him for support as he delivered his prepared speech. Sadly, David's words didn't reflect the wonderful things about Sam, only his perceived connection to her.

When the reception started winding down, I asked David if he would like to see the plaque in the church on which Sam's named would be engraved. He nodded and, along with his wife and children, accompanied me to the church. We found the plaque, and I promised to send a picture when Sam's name appeared on it. We all had a cordial chat that left me feeling hopeful of healing between David and me.

When we returned to the reception hall, almost everyone was gone. We sat at a table and I began eating cake. I continued eating cake for days—there was a lot leftover. I haven't had difficulty eating since.

David and his family left shortly afterward. Only a handful of Sam's friends remained, including Robert. These few friends joined Max and me outside as we released the colorful balloons and sent our love to Sam. This festive and beautiful sight made a perfect ending to Sam's life here.

MESSAGES FROM SAM: Sam described the reception as a much lighter event than the service and acknowledged it as a celebration with lots of laughter and stories. She liked it.[2] *She also wanted me to know that she was there when we released the balloons to her.*[3]

During another conversation, Sam surprised me when she lightheartedly admitted she was more loved in death than in life. She laughed about it, finding it funny that there were people who came to her funeral who weren't close to her. She said they came because they were caught up in the fascination of someone young dying.[4]

---

2. JD, December 21, 2018
3. JF, September 7, 2016
4. BH, Early 2018

Pokémon and Trees

In long-term relationships, we're continuously uncovering the quirks and flaws of our significant other. And if we are fortunate, we continue to discover wonderful qualities as well. When I started dating Max, his devotion to family and his willingness to help others stood out as major selling points to me. So, it was no surprise when he offered to drive to Sam's apartment in Orlando and pack up her belongings for me. He knew that Sam's apartment would be too harmful for me to breathe in, with scented products in all the living spaces. But he also probably knew that, at that time, I wouldn't be able to handle it emotionally.

Sam's many friends, upon their regular visits to the apartment, probably thought she kept every trinket, poster, piece of artwork, book, DVD, CD, video game, and souvenir from her entire life. And they would be right. But I would like to set the record straight: only half of her belongings were in her apartment. The other half were, and still are, in storage in Tallahassee. It took three days and two trips for Max to go through and retrieve all of Sam's apartment stuff.

Emma, Robert, and other close friends were helpful and claimed a few sentimental objects. Other than the coffee table we had given Sam, the furniture was left behind. All the rest came back with Max, stuffed into every available space in his car.

Exactly two weeks after Sam's passing, on the last day

of packing up the apartment, Max dropped by a memorial event in Orlando before heading home. Sam's Pokémon buddies were hosting a tournament to honor her. The event was both heartwarming and lively. The game room at Cool Stuff Games was filled with competitive players, food, and flower arrangements, which had been donated by Sam's floral shop family.

At the end of the tournament, a check was handed to Max for Sam's memorial fund. The tournament had an entry fee that was intended for this purpose, of which we were totally unaware. This additional gift blew me away. The extremely generous GoFundMe collection had paid for everything. Now, we had this extra money that we didn't know how to use.

It's hard for me to express how I felt receiving these donations. The thought of so many people honoring my daughter was overwhelming. To know that my child was loved by so many has been one of the greatest gifts of my life. But I also felt uncomfortable about being given something that was no longer needed. I wanted to say, "Thank you, from the bottom of my heart, but please take it back."

Then Avery, who'd helped organize the tournament, suggested we put the money toward other Pokémon tournaments. We loved the idea. It offered the perfect solution: returning the money, without actually handing it back. So, we tentatively planned to have an annual memorial Pokémon tournament.

Before the second annual tournament, we found another way to honor Sam that utilized some of the funds. We donated a tree on behalf of Sam's friends at a beautiful new park in Tallahassee. Max and I donated a second tree, and Max's family, a third. Two of the trees are Japanese magnolias and one is a Japanese maple. Sam loved everything Japanese, especially manga (comic books/novels), anime (animated shows/films), and of course, Pokémon. Each tree has a plaque on which Sam's name and a message are engraved.

The tree paid for by the tournament proceeds is dedicated to her memory by "Friends and family near and far."

Max and I hosted the tournament the following two years. Wearing a mask and a large lab coat for protection, I remained in the building for at least half of the time. We used up the last of the memorial fund on food and prizes at the third tournament, knowing that we probably wouldn't continue to host the event, as it was physically becoming too difficult for me.

I'm grateful that I was able to make the trip for both the second and third tournaments. Meeting players and experiencing the excitement of a Pokémon tournament gave me a glimpse into one of Sam's worlds.

MESSAGES FROM SAM: Sam thoroughly enjoyed watching the memorial Pokémon tournaments and thought they were "cool." I think this is because her friends were able to honor her while playing a game that they could connect to her. I asked Sam what she thought about us discontinuing the tournament. She quickly gave her approval, saying it had become overwhelming and unhealthy for me. Then she said, "It was part of the natural progression of grief. You needed to let go of that."[1]

Sam acknowledged that friends and family go to the place where her name appears on a plaque to visit her, as opposed to the gravesite. This is true. I previously learned that several people, who wanted a special place to talk to Sam, went to the park to be with her trees. Sam said she goes there often. And even though the park didn't exist when she was growing up, she now knows it well.[2]

---

1. JD, March 7, 2019
2. JD, December 11, 2018

A Furry World

One month after Sam's passing, another memorial event was held in Orlando to honor her. Max and I drove down for the day to attend. It took place during the annual furry convention called Megaplex, which Sam had attended every year since her first summer in Orlando. If you've ever been to a Star Trek or other fandom convention where the guests wear costumes, then you might be able to visualize what we experienced when we entered this fun-loving fantasy world.

Megaplex exists to provide art and entertainment for its guests, many of whom come in costume or full-body "fursuits." Just like the friendly animal characters at Disney World, there were lively personalities everywhere showing off their furry personas and wearing animal suits that they had created. Some made their own and others commissioned professionals to make them. And most fursuits looked just as impressive as those you would see

at Disney World. Sam didn't have a suit, but we learned she'd begun working on one with the assistance of one of her skilled furry friends.

MESSAGES FROM SAM: Sam described Megaplex as a place where she felt she could leave reality and "step into this whole other world"—a world where she felt comfortable, free, loved, and accepted. It was a place where she could be herself and have fun. She loved it! And even though she didn't have an animal suit, Sam said she did dress up a bit.[1]

When Max and I arrived, we were greeted outside by Sophie, who had come all the way from Boston. Sam and Sophie had met through the digital art community and had been communicating daily for more than a year. They had fallen in love and were trying to figure out their long-distance relationship. However, they had difficulty meeting up physically. I had never met Sophie but couldn't wait to embrace her. I knew immediately who she was when I saw her. A pretty girl with similarities to Sam, she appeared shy and a little nervous. The moment our arms wrapped around each other, I felt like I was holding Sam. I could sense Sophie's need to hold me, too. If I had left the convention right then and driven all the way back home, that one moment would have been worth the trip.

MESSAGES FROM SAM: Sam confirmed that she and Sophie didn't physically get together much because of the distance between Boston and Orlando. However, their connection was very strong, like kindred spirits, and they communicated all the time.[2]

Sam has expressed her gratitude for my continued correspondence with her friends.[3] And I believe she especially

---

1. JD, February 22, 2019
2. JD, February 22, 2019
3. BH, April 27, 2017

appreciated my interaction with Sophie, with whom I stayed in touch regularly for about three years. When she wrote, her words and thoughts sounded just like Sam. I felt so connected to Sophie, and our communication brought me great comfort.

Sophie directed us to the "Dealer's Den," where she had left her drawing supplies on a table that Sam had rented before her unexpected death. Many artists offer on-the-spot commissioned drawings at these conventions, and Sam, like Sophie, periodically provided custom artwork for furry guests. It had seemed like a good idea for Sophie to take Sam's place, so as to not let the rental go to waste. And Sophie admitted to needing the income.

Max and I sat and watched Sophie and other artists do what I had never been able to see Sam do. It amazed me. Even with my background in art, I couldn't imagine illustrating so quickly and so well.

Throughout the day, several of Sam's furry friends introduced themselves to us. As it got closer to the scheduled time of the memorial, we visited with some of Sam's Pokémon buddies, who looked as intrigued by the colorful characters and playful atmosphere as we were.

MESSAGES FROM SAM: As she further described this unique, furry "other world," Sam validated that she was in her comfort zone at these conventions, and her insecurities left her. Unprompted, she talked to strangers and was able to connect with a lot of people while she drew and sold her art.

Sam has assured me

that she was with Max and me as we met all her furry friends and caught up with others who came for the memorial event. She acknowledged that I could feel the love from everyone. And indeed, I did.[4]

Early in the evening, furry friends, artist friends, and local friends gathered in a conference room to share their love and stories of Sam. On display at the front of the room were approximately fifty illustrations of Sam's character Sammy Fox, drawn by fellow artists and friends. It's difficult

Chelsea Ferguson
Kaitlyn Smith

---

4. JD, February 22, 2019

to describe the incredible artwork that so many produced to honor Sam and say goodbye. The unspoken messages reflected in the drawings took my breath away.

Carly, a talented artist from Canada and one of Sam's close friends, had organized the memorial gathering. They had known each other for years through the digital art community and had been able to visit each other a few times. Carly had come a long way to offer closure to those who couldn't come to the Tallahassee service. Along with Carly, several people took turns standing up and sharing memories of Sam.

I wish I could say all the messages were heartwarming— or at least rated PG-13. But I'm glad some people felt comfortable enough to share inappropriate anecdotes, like those associated with having too much to drink.

MESSAGES FROM SAM: A few years after her passing, Sam interrupted a question I had about another memorial event. She wanted to talk about the lively gathering held at Megaplex. Sam playfully said, "What they said was so nice." And then she expressed a desire to give her buddies a

hard time for some of the things they said about her.[5]

Many of those present had been careful not to wear fragrances, and I stayed for at least half of the event. Eventually, though, I became lightheaded and my lungs severely irritated. I had no choice but to leave.

Max helped me get outside. After a while, I felt better and we decided to return to the conference room. Although the event had come to a close, Carly and Sophie were still there. To my surprise, Carly handed me all the drawings. What a gift!

As we hugged and said our goodbyes, I felt closure in another step of my grieving process.

---

5. JD, October 28, 2018

MESSAGES FROM SAM: It was obvious that Sam wanted to share her furry convention life with me from the other side. Her excitement came through as she talked about it at great length. She acknowledged that Max and I had gotten a glimpse of something we had known very little about. And she admitted the attendees were a "very interesting group of people." Then she said, "It definitely can get weird."[6]

---

6. JD, February 22, 2019

Medium Rare

The activity surrounding Sam's passing had kept me moving. But once the Orlando memorial was over, emptiness overcame me. I still had difficulty getting to sleep. I cried every night, until my head became so congested that I was too uncomfortable to fall asleep. But the mornings had changed. They were different from those in that first week. I no longer wanted to get out of bed.

If it weren't for the muscle pain, I might have stayed in bed for more than half of every day. Perhaps I should be grateful for the muscle cramps that develop during my sleep. I finally crawled out of bed when I couldn't stand the discomfort any longer.

A couple of weeks after Sam left, the condolence cards, messages, and visits ended. And then over the next couple of months, the support and understanding seemed to fade away. It was as if the world said, "Time's up. It's time to get back to the way things were." For those not affected by my daughter's death, this was understandable. But with the exception of Sam's friends, Max's family, and my stepmother, only two people got in touch during this time to check on me. The absence of supportive friends and family was a reminder of the desolate life I had been living.

It was Sam's friends who provided the most comfort. They communicated with me frequently. And I knew that I was giving them something too. In a way, they got to connect with a piece of Sam whenever they connected with me. But overall, I think they reached out to me because they were genuinely caring people.

After a few weeks of floundering, I began designing a printed book of all the incredible memorial artwork. The collection of drawings had grown since the Megaplex event. Sam's friends and fellow artists posted their art on Facebook, and a few sent me illustrations directly. I felt like the Grinch when his heart kept growing. I was as impressed by the exquisite work of the professional artists as I was by the creations of the non-artists, who put time, energy, and love into something that perhaps did not come easily for them.

The book of memorial artwork gave me purpose. I later modified it to include pictures of Sam throughout different stages of her life, as well as all the memorial events that had taken place that first year after she departed.

Between walking and making the book, I talked to Sam a lot. I wondered how often she was with me. At about three or four months after her passing, I started to feel lost. My life of solitude now felt devastatingly void. And I ached to hear Sam's voice and to hold her.

Max worked hard and sometimes for long hours. On weekends he caught up on chores and projects. And when he could arrange it, he would spend time with his girls. In addition to my heartache, he had his own family issues to handle. Sometimes, I felt more alone when he was home. I no longer felt like a person with value.

Occasionally, Max and I would go to a local bookstore, Books-A-Million. Given the building's constant air flow and high ceilings, I was able to stay a couple of hours if I wore a mask. Of course, I could have gone by myself, but I never knew when I might need Max's help escaping from an exposure. Also, it was nice to go somewhere together, even though we meandered our preferred aisles separately.

I usually spent most of my time browsing the spirituality section, looking for books on near-death experiences. Over the past decade, I'd read a handful of captivating books by people who'd had them. With my interest in Sam's life in heaven increasing, I wanted to read as much as I could from people who had actually visited the other side. I would grab a few books and read enough from each to feel uplifted. Once in a blue moon, a book would be worth purchasing.

One day, in the middle of my deep despair over losing Sam, I wandered into another section, looking for a specific book. I can't even remember what I was searching for at the time. However, I ended up staring at a display of books at the end of an aisle. Although I didn't like what I saw, it stopped me in my tracks.

The theme of the book display appeared to be New Age spirituality, and two books written by a celebrity medium caught my attention. I had briefly seen a clip of this medium's TV show, and her animated TV personality made me skeptical. I didn't know what I believed about mediums, but I had serious doubts about her authenticity. I moved on to look for something else.

A couple of weeks later, it happened again. I had no intention of going into that section, yet I found myself in front of the same display, staring at the pictures of this TV medium. Something inside me said, *It's okay, just take a quick look.* Maybe it was my curiosity. Maybe it was my yearning to communicate with Sam. Maybe it was someone else finally getting my attention. I started to read the first book written by the celebrity. I couldn't stop reading.

Instantly, I just knew this TV medium wasn't a fraud. And I knew I had to read the whole book. I bought it. And when I finished it, I returned for the second book. I thought, *Okay, now I believe in mediums. So how do I find someone like her? And how do I find a reputable medium who lives around here?*

My search led me to discover that countless people claim to have the ability to connect with spirits on the other side. Some are authentic. And what I found truly amazing is that these mediums can give messages over the phone. Really. They can. At first, I'd thought advertising that you could do a psychic reading over the phone was a true indicator that you were a con artist. But the more I learned, the more I discovered that our loved ones in spirit can talk to a medium anywhere in the world while also being with us. For example, Sam could be with me in my home while I listened to her messages via a medium in Timbuktu.

I began reading reviews. *Lots* of reviews. I finally found an online resource of hundreds of supposedly authentic mediums, which also included a short list of legitimate professionals who had been tested by the site's author.

Before finding this site, I tried out a couple of mediums who didn't charge much. But as with many things, you get what you pay for. Only a few images and words came through, and although some of the messages were specific to me—losing a child, for example—I didn't get any direct messages from Sam.

Then I tried one of the mediums on the preferred list of this particular website. Wow! Sam came through! Everything changed at that moment. I finally knew my Sammy could communicate with me. (Since then, I've had a couple of not-so-good readings with other reputable mediums who cost a pretty penny. I've also had great readings with mediums who charge affordable rates.)

This first great communication with Sam was made possible by a very gifted gentleman, Glenn Klausner, who has been aware of his abilities since the age of four. He is internationally known and offers readings over the phone.

MESSAGES FROM SAM: It would be an understatement to say that I was elated to finally hear from Sam. The comfort it brought me was unsurpassed. In this extraordinary session, Sam provided a variety of messages, presumably thoughts she had been waiting to share.

I loved how the session began. Being theatrical, Sam

made an elaborate and glamorous entrance. She showed herself elegantly dressed, descending a grand staircase. Surrounded by nine men, Sam was in the center. And on each side of her were two grandfathers: her paternal grandfather, Brad, and her maternal step-grandfather, Jack. The men were saying, "Sam gets it!" I presumed this meant she had completely transitioned and had the ability to connect via a medium. (I have since discovered that some spirits communicate much better with humans than others.)

Of the many topics she covered, Sam wanted me to know she'd been spending time with Jack, my mom's second husband. In this life, Sam had been as close to Jack as she had my dad, who was still living at the time. She joked about him playing poker and gambling. This really hit home with me, since Jack had loved playing poker here and had hosted a weekly game for years. Sam teased that she wouldn't go to Las Vegas with him because he was a high roller. "He either wins three times as much, or he loses."[1] When I later asked Sam to clarify what she meant by this, she said that spirits can get into a person's energy—not take over—and feel the rush of rolling the dice or contemplating the cards. And they help the person intuitively pick and choose what to do. They don't cheat. It's fun for them to guess like we do. When Sam said "wins three times as much," she basically meant Jack helped someone win three times more than they bet.[2]

Sam also said she took Jack to a spa, and being playful, told him, "I'm paying! Let's have a good time." This wouldn't have been something Jack would have done as an earthly man. The two of them got exfoliated, had massages and facials, and then had their nails done. At the time, I wondered how they could experience this, but I now know spirits in heaven can do whatever they want.

Sam delivered her messages at top speed, and the

---

1. GK, November 16, 2015
2. JB, November 9, 2020

medium did a remarkable job keeping up. Although Sam could talk fast when she was alive, it wasn't a defining characteristic. She mentioned checking in on friends and family here, especially her father. She followed by saying the value of people is all the same. And we need to see our own self-worth. Then she added, "We only focus on good here."

She also shared some words of wisdom, such as, "A smile on the face keeps the doctor away," and that we need to listen to our hearts, not our heads.

Admitting that she'd been shy here, she proclaimed that this is not the case in heaven. And she divulged that she and I would be working on a project together to help others. She also said one of her missions is to empower people. And she playfully revealed that I would be rewarded for getting a message to a particular family member. "You'll get extra brownie points for this." Then she added that there are charts and records kept on the other side.

Sam wrapped up by giving me a little more insight into her afterlife. She told me she "lives in joy." What uplifting words! She reminded me that she is always with me, and although I didn't feel it, she gave me a hug.[3]

---

3. GK, November 16, 2015

Max the Skeptic

I share almost everything with Max. So when I started connecting with Sam, I wanted to pass on every fascinating message to him. Unfortunately, he was even more skeptical about mediums than I had been.

I could sense that it was difficult for him to believe the communications were truly from Sam. However, being the supportive and thoughtful man that he is, he didn't discourage me from trying to connect with Sam in this way.

Every once in a while, I would provide Max with bits of information that validated the messages actually came from Sam. But inevitably, later, he would suggest that he still wasn't convinced it was possible to converse with heaven.

So, one night I asked him what he wanted me to ask Sam in my session with a medium the next day. After dwelling on the matter, and thinking he was being clever, he requested that I ask her what new animal she'd been playing with. And then Max announced to the room—hoping Sam would hear—that he wanted her to say "rhino." In other words, he wanted me to ask his question, but regardless of the correct answer, he wanted her to say "rhino."[1]

First of all, let me say that Sam hates being tested. This was her personality in this life, as well. Fortunately for me, every now and then she throws out some validation to warm my heart, or just to see my reaction, or both. I love it when

---

1. JD, December 31, 2019

she does this! However, I thought Max's request was a little much. He wanted her to give an answer that probably wasn't the truth, just to confirm her presence.

Max picked the rhinoceros as his test for Sam because he considers it to be his spirit animal. Now, when Max says spirit animal, he means the animal that he believes resembles his character. He has told me time and time again that he is a rhinoceros. I presume this is because he's a tough and solid guy—unmovable.

MESSAGES FROM SAM: As per Max's request, the next day, I asked Sam if she was playing with any new animals. At first, the medium looked confused. Sam had provided an image of a dusty, dirty rhino getting up from the ground.

I was thrilled! But the medium added that the rhino appeared quite a distance away. So I asked Sam if she was playing with it. She said, "Observing," implying this image was just for Max's benefit. Although rhinos aren't going to hurt her over there, she said she doesn't really have fun with them. However, she made the point that she would walk right up to one and touch it.

Spirit Animals

I then asked Sam if the rhinoceros was in fact Max's spirit animal. She confirmed that this was true. And she said that any time we feel connected or drawn to an animal, there's something in the animal's energy that we need, and therefore it would be considered a spirit animal. She added that some of us have more than one and that they can change throughout our lifetime.

Using this new information, I decided to test my intuition. I asked her about my spirit animal. Over the past few years, I have admired the grace of gazelles and wondered if I had a connection to them.

Sam responded quickly. She said that right now, my

spirit animal was a deer. I thought I'd done fairly well. I consider a deer to be similar to a gazelle. Sam also said my animal changes more often than that of most people.

I was pleasantly shocked that Sam had entertained Max's request by giving him just what he had wanted. But to let him know that she'd been aware of his validity test, she concluded our spirit animal discussion by saying, "Tell Max, I just said..." Then she stuck out her tongue and blew a raspberry. As we were wrapping up our conversation that day, Sam said, "Make sure you tell Max for me..." and then she stuck out her tongue again and blew.[2] I have no doubt she followed this with a huge smile.

Many times, Sam has mentioned Max in her messages. During the first year after her passing, she wanted me to know what she really thinks of him. She said she loves him dearly and appreciates all that he did for her when she was

---

2. JD, December 31, 2019

here.[3] *And once she described him as "brilliant."*[4]

After hearing about the rhino episode, combined with the fact that he also believes he's brilliant, Max is no longer skeptical about Sam's communications through mediums.

---

3. GK, May 24, 2016
4. GK, November 16, 2015

New Kids on the Block

At the end of that first difficult summer without Sam, I assessed the emptiness in my life and realized I needed someone or something else to nurture and love. When Sam was alive, I had believed I would always be needed, no matter what stage of her life she was in. But now, I no longer was needed.

I decided to adopt a dog. After weeks of visiting shelters and a couple of animal foster homes, I found the perfect fit: a young and gentle black lab. She seemed to be "the one." The day I planned to pick her up from the center, I called to ask a couple of questions. But someone told me my dog had already been adopted. *What?* I had already agreed to take the dog. Apparently, someone had seen her before me, so they had the right to take her if they arrived first.

I couldn't believe this had happened. And I couldn't believe how invested my heart had become after just a few days. I felt lost. Again.

A few days later, I picked myself up and started looking again. It took a while, but I found another female dog, an adorable yellow lab puppy. Before it was too late, though, I decided she didn't feel right for me. I started worrying about her having to permanently stay outside. Because of my health problems, I needed living spaces that remained clean—but I felt outdoor dogs needed an outdoor companion. And two dogs felt like too much for me.

Confused, disappointed, and depressed, I wondered, *Am I not meant to have something to care for and love?*

Seeing my sadness, day after day, Max made an unexpected suggestion. "Let's get goats!" He had owned goats at his previous home, a farm in South Georgia. According to him, they were great pets and would take care of the lawn. He would never have to worry about mowing again. I trusted him.

By the end of September, Max and I were the proud parents of two goats. George, mostly African Pygmy, is a stunning male. And Butter is a plain, short-legged female, who appears to be mostly Nigerian Dwarf. They were adults but still young. We had hoped for a pair of kids, but none had been available in a small- to medium-size breed. Tallahassee doesn't have much of a farm-animal market.

We decided to let them mate in the hopes Butter would have one or two kids. She had given birth before, so we felt her experience could be helpful to us.

We soon realized how smart Butter is; George, not so much. He reminds me of a dumb brute—strong and aggressive but clueless. He also loves attention. It took Butter months to warm up to us, but I'm now her favorite human. She comes to me more than once a day to be petted, and she lets me clean the goo out of the corners of her eyes, even though she doesn't like the way it feels. George and Max have bonded—they like to play rough. The goats definitely know that I'm the softie and Max is the tough guy.

It didn't take long for Butter to get pregnant. In the spring of 2016, she went into labor. Thank goodness I had studied goat deliveries beforehand—apparently Butter wasn't as experienced as we had thought. One of the kids wasn't breathing after delivery, and I had to assist. Fortunately, I had read up on how to handle this situation. And it worked!

Both kids were male. Looking for more fun in our lives, we named the babies Peanut and Jelly. Now we had Peanut,

Butter, and Jelly—and George, of course.

Jelly, the kid I saved at birth, was treated differently by Butter. After one month of nursing, she pushed him away. Although I didn't want to play favorites, I gave Jelly extra attention to comfort him. Peanut was born smaller, yet he grew to be the biggest and became aggressive at times. Jelly has been gentle since day one, and he's truly become *my* pet. I'm so glad that I was there to help bring him into this world. And I'm immensely grateful for our unique bond.

Though they've required a lot of care, our goats have brought us much joy and fulfillment.

MESSSAGES FROM SAM: Soon after getting Butter and George, I asked Sam what she thought of our new pets. She replied, "They're different! Nothing you do surprises me."[1] At the time, I was disappointed that was all she offered. But since the kids' birth, she has talked more about the goats and encouraged me to keep them. She said I need them and they need me.[2]

Sam finally admitted that she likes the goats. She thinks they're funny.[3] And she acknowledged their different personalities.[4] She also said they're smart, and they know their names when I call them.[5]

---

1. CL, January 2016
2. BH, March 2018
3. JD, March 29, 2019
4. GK, Early 2017; BH, Early 2018; JD, March 29, 2019
5. JD, February 2, 2019; JD, February 8, 2020

During one conversation about the goats, Sam confirmed that Jelly and I have a bond that goes beyond this life. Apparently, he's connected to my soul family on the other side.[6] Some animals form bonds with us on the soul level, just as people do, and they want to come into a life where they can be with us.[7]

Sam explained that Jelly has been around humans before in other lives. According to Sam, he and I have had multiple lives together. In one life, he was my horse. She said I rode him to travel, and we had a close bond.[8] She also said that he has his own way of thinking and doing things. I loved hearing this, because Jelly does in fact have

---

6. GK, Early 2017; JD, September 8, 2020
7. JD, September 8, 2020
8. JD, November 18, 2018; JD, September 8, 2020

unique characteristics.

In two different communications with Sam, my spirit guides interrupted us to inform me of problems with the goats. The first time this happened, I was told that one of my goats had gotten into something that harmed it and I needed to check on it.[9]

Following the session, I went outside and found all the goats looking healthy. But then I noticed Butter limping. I called her over, and she willingly allowed me to pick up her foot. An inch of a stick was protruding from her hoof. Disturbed, I pulled it out as quickly as I could. The stick came out—and to my horror, it was four inches long. She was fine from that point, and I could sense her gratitude.

The other warning dealt with a digestion issue. Before this conversation, I had known it was about time to deworm the goats, and I'd noticed that Jelly was lethargic. So after hearing my guide's warning, we purchased and administered the dewormer.[10] A couple of weeks later, when Jelly looked happy and healthy, I was told the goats were all fine.[11]

More on Animals

Twice, Sam has tried to explain to me what communication with animals is like on the other side. Spirits and animals—including fish—exchange thoughts telepathically. But they don't have deep conversations.[12] Sam teasingly said it's not like getting together over a cup of coffee and having a chat. She says the gist of the communication with animals is an expression of appreciation and love.[13]

More than once, I've been reminded that animals are a

---

9. JD, March 18, 2019; JD, March 29, 2019
10. JD, August 6, 2020
11. JD, September 8, 2020
12. JD, September 14, 2019
13. JD, October 1, 2020

gift to us here. Through their love for us, animals offer emotional support and healing. And to my surprise, animals on the other side also provide healing to spirits in heaven. Sam said animals can help with the transition of spirits coming in and out of human lives, especially spirits who are disoriented when they first arrive on the other side. Animals bring comfort and healing while these spirits get their bearings.[14]

Arrival home is also different for animals. In general, when humans cross over, everybody we know and love is waiting for us. It's like a reunion. But for animals, there's no reunion or period of adjustment. They just find themselves among all the other spirits, both people and animals. Their life in heaven isn't that much different than it was on earth—just better. And because there's no animal abuse on the other side, animals only experience love.

If we have a strong bond with an animal, we can choose to come into another life with it. It will be part of our plan. And even though the animal will want this, we will make this choice, not the animal.[15] *And just like Jelly, my goat, animals can return here as different species.*[16]

---

14. JD, October 1, 2020
15. JD, September 14, 2019
16. JD, February 6, 2020

Wrong Time to Cry

On Sammy's first birthday following her passing, I briefly woke as the sun started to rise. I looked at my clock to see a time that made no sense at all—too early for daylight. I figured that either the batteries needed to be changed or I needed to buy a new clock, and I fell back asleep.

Later that day, when I finally got out of bed, I realized there was a good chance that Sam had been messing with my clock. I felt exhilarated. How cool would that be? I reset my clock, to see what would happen. Nothing unusual; it worked perfectly and continued to work for months and months until it finally needed new batteries.

As the day unfolded, it seemed like any other day. I had expected it to be tough, but the clock episode had lifted my spirits and reminded me Sam was, and would be, with me. I looked forward to the evening, when Max and I would celebrate Sam's twenty-fifth birthday by eating cake from our favorite cake shop. She and I both loved chocolate and vanilla marble cake with fudge frosting. When Max got home from work, my mother joined us in singing "Happy Birthday" to Sam before we indulged in the yummy cake.

Seeing the wrong time on the clock had reminded me that her birthday wasn't a time to cry but a time to cherish her life here. It became the first of Sam's special days that I've chosen to celebrate.

MESSAGES FROM SAM: Three years after that significant day, I asked Sam if she'd messed with my alarm clock on one of her birthdays. She quickly responded that on the first birthday after her departure, she knew how difficult it would be for me. She said, "It was a big day, so I wanted to let you know I was around." She only had to touch the clock and her energy interfered.[1]

Following this exciting confirmation of her intervention, Sam reminded me that she can easily manipulate electrical and battery-operated devices.[2] Since then, Sam has messed with my alarm clock several times. Once, during a partially sleepless night, she turned it off. I discovered this before it was time to get up, so I reset it. But she turned it off again and I overslept. When I asked her about this, Sam said she did it because I needed more sleep.[3]

Another night, when I was sick, Sam altered the time on my clock. I remember feeling grateful when I woke up the next morning and saw the wrong time. I needed something to cheer me up. Like a nurturing mother, Sam said she had attempted to make me more comfortable during the night. She'd given me kisses and rearranged my sheets and pillow. To verify her actions, she described her location as being next to my pillow and mentioned there was a picture of a bird above my head—which there was.

When the medium expressed her concern about Sam interfering with my alarm clock so often, Sam reassured her that it has never bothered me. "I know she likes that."[4]

Oh, I do!

---

1. JD, December 21, 2018; JD, June 15, 2019
2. JD, December 21, 2018
3. JD, April 25, 2019
4. JD, June 25, 2019

The Christmas Gift

Getting through the Christmas holidays that first year proved difficult, but I'd expected as much. I knew I would miss the activities that Sam and I loved doing together, like baking cookies, watching our favorite Christmas movies, playing games, and exchanging presents chosen with great thought and love. And I knew that my heart would be heavy when I woke up without Sam on Christmas Day.

To keep my spirits up, Sloan—my sweetheart of a niece, who was on holiday break from college—came over a few days before Christmas and baked cookies with me. We used Sam's favorite frosted sugar cookies recipe. I will forever be grateful for the time Sloan shared with me that first Christmas. It filled an emptiness and was a special visit for the two of us.

Sloan, who is a couple of years younger than Sam, is now a nurse. Even though she and Sam didn't get together often, they had a close bond. They both have the same compassionate spirit and are wonderful examples of people who express genuine kindness to everyone.

Max usually celebrated the holidays with his girls the week following December 25, so he had nothing tying him to our Christmas in Tallahassee. I wanted to get as far away as possible on that day and escape the memories of Christmases with Sam. I thought Italy would be nice. Not possible, but nice. I suggested Epcot in Disney World—we could spend Christmas Day traveling from one country to another, including Italy, enjoying different cultures and their festivities.

Max thought it was a healthy idea, at least emotionally. We knew that it might be too physically challenging for me, but we were both willing to take the risk.

On a beautiful and mild winter day, we spent hours in Epcot. The crowds did indeed cause me harm at times, but I did my best to work around them and Max tried to be patient. I especially enjoyed the choir presentation and the narration of the Christmas story at the end of the day. We sat at the very back of the amphitheater and for a moment, the day felt like Christmas. I'm glad we made the trip.

On the second Christmas after Sam's death, something out of this world happened. In the winter, I turn on a space heater in the morning when my alarm goes off. While the heater gets going, I hit snooze and go back to sleep. I proceed to wake up and hit snooze every five minutes until the room is warm enough to get out of bed.

But on that Christmas morning, the heater was already on when I woke up. And the room was at the optimal temperature. No one had been in my room but me. And I *never* leave the heater on at night. If I did, my room would be a deadly inferno by morning.

I knew Sam had done it. Filled with joy, I cried.

MESSAGES FROM SAM: Every year before the holidays, Sam reminds me that she'll be with me at Christmas. Of course, I know this. She's with me whenever I think of her. Plus, she knows how special our past Christmases together were. I believe her reminders are just to let me know how much she thinks about me.[1]

When I asked Sam if she did anything special for me on that second Christmas, she confirmed that she had turned

---

1. JF, September 7, 2016; SH, October 2017

on the heater.² *She said it took a long time to plan: "I had to prepare. That was time consuming for me."* And she had to enlist the help of guides because she couldn't physically manipulate the buttons. She also acknowledged that I had cried. *"You teared up."* And then she said, *"It was a Christmas gift."*³ As she shared this, I couldn't help but cry again.

---

2. GK, January 2, 2017; JD, October 5, 2018
3. JD, October 5, 2018

A Hard Day's Knight

Once a year, the University of Central Florida holds its Eternal Knights Ceremony to honor students who have passed away during the previous twelve months. Unaware of this memorial event, I received an invitation in the mail. When I called UCF to find out more about the ceremony, I learned that the only mention of my daughter would be her name and major.

I debated whether to make the trip to Orlando just to hear a generic service that would bestow upon Sam the distinction of "Eternal Knight." Two considerations helped me make my decision. First, Sam's Orlando buddies and her cousin, Sloan, would easily be able to attend. And second, I might regret it later if I didn't go. I chose to go.

Happy to be sharing another event with Sam's closest friends and Sloan, I invited them to sit with Max and me in the front row as family. Sloan, Robert, and two other friends, Stacy and Jeff, gladly accepted the honor. And to my surprise, all of Sam's animation classmates, as well as the professor, left their classwork to attend.

The ceremony began quietly and ended quietly. A dreary reverence filled the air. I sensed an intended message: honoring our deceased children as "Eternal Knights" should lessen our grief. But it didn't for me, and I doubt it did for others. I saw such sadness on the faces of the other parents. Even though I knew that the grief will never end for me, I realized that some of the parents had lost their children recently. By this point, my own sadness came and went. I had been dealing with it for nine months.

The worst part of the ceremony was when Sam's name and major were announced. Yep, that was it. Nothing important or special was mentioned. I had prepared myself for this, but the incompleteness of the ceremony still disappointed me.

At the end of the ceremony, a woman stood up and sang. I presume she was some sort of staff or faculty because she didn't sound like a professional vocalist. Her vocal range didn't quite fit the song. Suddenly, I was reminded of the times I'd been in school or church when something funny hit me but it was inappropriate to laugh. Trying to suppress it made me want to laugh more or even louder.

In the darkened room, while the woman sang meaningful lyrics to a powerful tune, I started laughing in my head. The urge to laugh out loud grew, until it took all I had to contain myself. I decided to talk to Sam, in my head, hoping it would be a distraction. I asked if she felt I was being disrespectful for having critical thoughts about the performance. No answer came.

Finally, the song was over, and I recovered. To me, this part of the program made the event. It certainly lifted my spirits. After the ceremony, I visited with some of Sam's classmates before moving into an adjoining reception room for the families of the deceased students. Sam's close friends and Sloan also attended the reception. Large round tables filled the room, and our group took up almost an entire table. We chatted and laughed, having our own little celebration. I felt a bit uncomfortable for the other parents.

At that time, the "Sam Book," as I called it, included pictures of everyone at the table and all the memorial artwork. I had brought a copy for everyone in our "family" at the table. Flipping through the pages brought back great memories for everyone. While viewing the artwork in the book, Stacy and Jeff decided to share their newest artistic creations dedicated to Sam—tattoos of Sammy Fox.

Before leaving, I spoke with a mother who had recently lost her son. I'm glad I did. The women felt so alone, even though her husband was there. She admitted that her husband still struggled with overwhelming grief. I learned that they had another son, and for a moment, I envied the woman. Only briefly, though.

MESSAGES FROM SAM: When I asked Sam about the memorial ceremony at the university, she started talking about the singing. She said the woman wasn't very good and acknowledged hearing everything I said to her in my head. Then Sam shocked me by saying she was egging me on, which probably contributed to my extreme discomfort. She wanted me to burst out laughing, just to lighten the mood.[1]

---

1. JD, October 26, 2018

Final Films

As promised, I did make it to the presentation of the Final Films produced by Sam's animation class. And although she wasn't there with me physically, Sam definitely was present. Max and Sloan accompanied me. We brought food from home and had a picnic outside beforehand.

Overlooking my masked face, the students and faculty welcomed us and shared their memories of Sam. She had worked with her film team a whole year, and they had become a close-knit group. They explained Sam's contributions and showed us the animation labs. One had been named after her. A plaque had been placed outside the lab next to the door. It's hard to put into words the emotions I felt when I saw Sam's name as a permanent fixture in the animation department. It was another comforting statement of the affection so many had for Sam.

The theater-style classroom where the films were being shown was packed that night. Max, Sloan, and I sat at the very top. And although I experienced some distress from the fragrances around me, I managed to make it to the end of the showings. Before the films played, a professor addressed the families and friends who had come to witness the students' accomplishments. She also announced that both films had been dedicated to Sam, and then she acknowledged my and Max's presence there.

The short film created by Sam's team told a humorous

story about a meticulous college student eagerly awaiting the arrival of a new dorm mate. (I got excited when I spotted a couple of items in the dorm room that Sam had created.) To the surprise of the student, a human girl, her new roommate was a moth. The moth deliberately instigated chaos, which led to the destruction of the immaculate room and prompted the girl's departure. Delighted his plan had worked, the moth invited all his buddies to enjoy his new quarters.

MESSAGES FROM SAM: When I asked Sam about the night of the Final Films, she showed off by sending an image of the plaque that had been installed in her honor.

Following her verification of being honored, Sam reported on the event. "It went beautifully." She did acknowledge, however, that it had been difficult for me. And she took credit for protecting me so that I could survive all the fragrances and experience the whole evening.

Wanting to emphasize her participation in her team's film, Sam stated, "That was my film." She confirmed that her name had been included in the credits. And then she described black-and-white illustrations at the end of the film that preceded a dedication and picture of her.[1]

After hearing this, I played the film (a DVD had been sent to me) to see what she was talking about. And there at the end were black-and-white line figures dancing, right before the dedication appeared.

---

1. JD, February 22, 2019; JD, September 3, 2020

European Escape

A couple of years after Sam left, I suggested to Max that we take another trip to Italy. He didn't need much prodding. Either he wanted to go as badly as I did, or he saw that I desperately needed to escape. We decided to include Southern France in our travels this time as well.

France has always been a country of interest to me. I studied the language in school, and my father's ancestors were French. But the main reason I wanted to visit France had more to do with Sam.

MESSAGES FROM SAM: According to conversations with Sam via five different mediums, she and I lived our most recent life together in France. All of these messages relayed the same information: We were mother and daughter, and Sam was the child. We lived near Nice, in the region of Provence. And we were both alive during the 1920s.[1]

At a very young age in that life, I got pregnant with Sam. There wasn't a father figure during her childhood. Because we grew up together, our bond went beyond a typical mother-daughter relationship. We had a very strong connection.[2]

Sam has shown an image of the two us from that life,

---
1. BH, April 27, 2017; SH, January 30, 2019; JD, February 7, 2019; VD, March 15, 2019; JB, November 9, 2020
2. JD, February 7, 2019; JD, May 4, 2020; JB, November 9, 2020

when she was a child. It was a great moment. We were riding a bicycle built for two.³ At the front, I was pedaling, and Sam was on the back seat with her legs sticking out, enjoying the free ride.⁴

But this life wasn't an easy one. I came from a poor family, and we had to work hard for everything we had. However, Sam wanted me to know that the most significant part about that life, and all the other lives we've experienced, was what we learned. She said, "Don't be so concerned about the specifics, because over here, it's a collective of everything we know. Focus more on the relationships and what you've learned."

So, I asked Sam to share what we learned in that life. She adamantly replied, "Survival." And then she added "companionship and trust," because we had to rely on each other so much. "No life do we ever have just one thing." There are always several lessons. Sometimes, there's a stronger theme in a life. And in that life, as with others, it was survival.⁵

Having survived the flight, my biggest challenge, we spent the first four days on an organic farm in Southwest France, near a town called Najac. The peaceful and beautiful scenery immediately melted away the stress we had carried from home.

MESSAGES FROM SAM: After the trip, I downloaded our pictures onto my computer. I was thrilled when I saw orbs in a handful of them. I knew what this meant. Orbs in photos that aren't due to lighting irregularities are spirits. The pictures had been taken in our bedroom on our last morning in Najac. The photos captured a large window, with its magical view of the countryside, and orbs in

---

3. MG, November 1, 2019; JB, November 9, 2020
4. MG, November 1, 2019
5. JD, February 7, 2019

two corners of the room.

Sam has taken credit for these. She has also said teasingly that if the resolution of the images had been better, I would have been able to see her "little face" in the orbs. I found this amusing, but I wasn't sure if she was just having fun with me or not.

Next, we spent eleven nights at a huge organic farm in Tuscany, in the province of Pisa. While staying there, we ventured to several historic hilltop towns in the surrounding area and revisited popular cities, such as Florence and Siena.

The landscapes were spectacular, and the people were warm and welcoming. In both France and Italy, we bought fresh food at small butcher shops and grocery stores in the nearby towns. Cooking fresh local food is always the most rewarding part of our European travels.

MESSAGES FROM SAM: As mentioned before, Sam confirmed that Italy felt like home to me, which made perfect sense. She has revealed that we've both lived several lives in Italy—more than in France.[6] Prior to my and Max's trip, she offered the names of four of the places I'd lived in that I would be able to visit while in Tuscany: Siena, Florence, Travalle, and the province of Pistoia.[7] Sam also said I had lived near Milan, but that was too far for this trip.[8]

To my delight, I discovered that our lodging and most of the sites we visited were either in the province of Pistoia or nearby. There are many charming hilltop towns throughout the region. It was a surreal but enjoyable experience to visit towns and cities where I've lived other lives. I felt a strong

---

6. JD, May 9, 2019; JD, September 3, 2020
7. BH, April 27, 2017; GK, July 7, 2017; SH, July 8, 2017
8. GK, July 7, 2017

connection with the countryside and towns I visited, but I can't say I felt a past-life bond with any place in particular.

Although we made it to the almost nonexistent town of Travalle, Sam later told me there was another Travale (spelled with only one "l") in Tuscany—the actual town I lived in during that past life. I'll definitely include it in a future trip.[9]

I asked Sam about some other orbs I saw, in pictures I took of the Baptistery of San Giovanni, the oldest religious structure in Florence. She confirmed that a lot of spirits hang out there and the energy is intense in that building.[10] Sam then shared something I never would have considered: a few centuries ago, in another life, I was baptized there.[11]

Near the end of our stay in Italy, we visited Siena. This city was special to me even before I took Sam there three years earlier. I'd even used it as the primary Italian town in my first screenplay. In the summer of 1979, while studying in Italy as part of an art program, I spent a day in Siena. It's a day I'll remember forever. While waiting on the famous Palio horse race that would take place that afternoon, I wandered the streets of a small neighborhood alone. A young Italian man befriended me and escorted me to the blessing of his community's horse in their chapel. It was truly an honor and an incredible experience.

MESSAGES FROM SAM: *Sam briefly mentioned the life we lived in Siena. She said we lived "just outside," on the east side of town. Even then, Siena was a busy area. We were both female, and we were extremely close friends.*[12]

Recently, Sam has brought up another life we lived in Siena. I was a young married woman who lived inside the

---

9. JD, March 5, 2020
10. JD, March 7, 2019
11. JD, March 7, 2019; JD, September 3, 2020; JB, November 9, 2020
12. JD, January 8, 2019

city. I would visit the vineyard of my father-in-law outside of Siena. On this property, there was a young boy whose father worked as hired help. This boy was Sam. Seeking companionship, I would spend time with the boy. Once, I dressed him up like a girl and took him to town. No one could tell he wasn't a girl. Giggling throughout the day, we had a spectacular time. Sam said this was a very theatrical life.[13]

Near the small town of Solliès-Toucas, in Provence, Max and I spent our last week in a two-bedroom villa. Although located in the mountains, the villa was only forty-five minutes north of the French Riviera. If it weren't for the head cold that Max had caught and then gave to me, we would have experienced more than we did. Max soldiered through his cold quickly, and he was in great shape by the time we reached France. I, on the other hand, felt miserable.

Still, we visited several beaches, and popular coastal towns such as St. Tropez, Marseille, Monaco, and Nice. For a large city, Nice is amazingly attractive. It captured my heart. Although located on the coast, it has a picturesque backdrop formed by the foothills of the Alps.

Max also loved Nice. We walked and walked, taking it all in.

MESSAGES FROM SAM: *Sam and I have lived a handful of lives together in France. It seems that almost all of them were in the southeast region.*[14] *And we were females in most of those lives since both of our souls identify more with female characteristics.*[15]

Sam disclosed why she prefers to be a female: "I don't like the aggression that comes with being a man on earth." She also revealed, "We tend to evolve quicker when we are

---

13. JB, November 9, 2020
14. GK, July 7, 2017; JD, September 7, 2018; JD, January 8, 2019
15. JD, September 7, 2018

females. Not that men don't evolve and not that they can't evolve quickly." She said so much more gets in the way for a male in the human form than it does for women.[16]

There was one lifetime we lived in Nice as males. Sam was my father. It was a simple time, with lots of outdoor activities. We fished a lot. She suggested I refer to The Andy Griffith Show to get an idea of our relationship. "That was kind of how we were. We didn't know technology like we do today, obviously. But it was the simple joys, like, 'This is how you catch a fish... you put a bait on the line...'" She told me it was a wonderful relationship.[17]

When I think about the many lifetimes Sam and I have planned and lived together, it reaffirms the deep and unbreakable connection we have. Each time she mentions one of our past lives, it brings a sense of comfort, as well as amusement.

---

16. JD, March 18, 2019
17. GK, October 12, 2017

Lullabies

~~~~~

For the past five years, I've had a nighttime ritual—when I get into bed, I talk to Sam. And somewhere along the line, I started asking her to sing me to sleep.

I still do this. Although I can't hear her, the idea of her sending me nurturing energy calms me. It reminds me of all the times I sang to her when she was a baby.

Sometimes, I sing too. Even though Sam could be singing at the same time, I doubt she minds. I like the idea of us singing together.

MESSAGES FROM SAM: Out of the blue, during a session one day, Sam asked the medium to confirm that she does indeed sing to me. "Tell her I come at night and I sing a lullaby." I was thrilled to hear this. I finally had confirmation that Sam sings to me at night.[1]

A couple of weeks later, I asked Sam which lullabies she sings. She said it's the same song every night—a French song. The medium admitted to not understanding French. I asked Sam to give us something in English. Instead, she showed an image of an old bridge.[2] *I researched and found a popular children's song titled "Sur le Pont d'Avignon," about people dancing on their town's bridge. The town, Avignon, is located in Provence, where Sam and I have lived at*

---

1. JD, August 17, 2018
2. JD, September 7, 2018

least two lives together, including our most recent one.

I thought it was sweet that Sam had been singing me a lullaby to help me fall asleep. But then I learned that "Sur le Pont d'Avignon" is an upbeat song. So "lullaby" is just Sam's playful word for singing me to sleep. When I later asked Sam to verify I had found the right song, she did.[3]

A month after Sam shared that she sings to me at night, she said that she occasionally dances around my room or acts out the lyrics. "Sometimes when I'm singing, I like to act out the song." She also sings "Tearin' Up My Heart," by NSYNC (she just likes the song and the beat), and an Italian love song.[4]

A few months later, Sam brought up the lullabies with another medium. She flashed musical notes and said they were the "lullabies" that she sings to me. Confused, the medium wondered why Sam called them that. Sam went on to explain that she'd been "returning the favor."[5] Wow! That touched me. I presume she was referring to my singing to her when she was a baby.

At that time, Sam revealed that she'd added a fourth song to rotate in with the other lullabies. But she didn't say which song.[6] Two months later, I asked her if there were any new songs. She responded, "I have not switched up my playlist." And although she said there would be more in the future, she said there was a reason why she sings the same songs over and over. The more she does the same thing, the more I will feel the connection. Also, she told me it could be disorienting if the energy she sends is constantly changing.[7]

When I asked her about the lullabies a year after she

---

3. JD, September 21, 2018
4. JD, October 26, 2018; JD, November 9, 2018
5. VD, March 15, 2019
6. JD, March 18, 2019
7. JD, May 9, 2019

first mentioned them, Sam reiterated, "I have a playlist."[8] And she acknowledged that she still dances around my room when she sings. Being cute, Sam joked, "I have to be careful not to knock your stuff over, though." And to show how silly she truly is, she showed a huge alpine horn that she sometimes plays to announce her lullaby. Sam finally shared a little more about the fourth lullaby—one of Aretha Franklin's well-known upbeat songs. The medium recognized the tune but couldn't remember the name. "It's fun," Sam added.[9] After two years of singing to me, and via a different medium, Sam confirmed the playlist had not changed—there were still only four songs.[10]

A few times, I thought I heard a couple of song lines in my head. Sam said that telepathy is the best way to communicate with humans. "It's easier when it just goes into your brain, like you think it's your own thing. Otherwise, it scares the shit out of most of you." Sam also revealed that singing in heaven is mostly telepathic.[11]

---

8. JD, September 18, 2019
9. JD, September 18, 2019
10. JB, November 9, 2020
11. JD, August 1, 2019

All Kinds of Love

Of all the dreams I had for Sam while she was alive, the dream that she would find love was the biggest. She craved to be with that special someone—the person she could love and who would love her back. When she first departed, I knew Sam would be surrounded by love. But I had no clue whether romantic love existed in heaven. And it definitely didn't occur to me that an equivalent to sex was there, too.

MESSAGES FROM SAM: Apparently, both romance and sex do exist on the other side.[1] Romantic affection, or intimacy, is an exchange of energy. "It's better than what you can experience as a human."[2] Sam described it as "a merging of energies. Very euphoric." Since spirits don't have physical bodies in heaven, they merge their energy to express and receive love. And the levels of the exchanged energy vary. Once spirits reach the level of euphoria they desire, they separate.

Sam also said that the exchanges aren't planned. "It's not a big deal." Spirits just know when they want to express themselves this way. And then she shocked me by saying, "It's definitely not a monogamous thing that happens over here."

---

1. JD, May 13, 2019; JD, October 11, 2019; JD, April 13, 2020
2. JD, May 13, 2019; JD, July 16, 2019

I asked Sam about whether spirits can kiss on the other side. She basically said it's the same as merging for sex, but less intense. Although it feels like touching each other, spirits can't actually touch each other physically. She reiterated, "When nobody has the physical human body, that's how we can feel each other."[3]

Sam emphasized the fact that we learn how to be intimate before we come here. "If there was no such thing as romantic love over here, you guys wouldn't know what to do when you got there. As far as love goes, love is all that exists over here." And she added, "There's all kinds of love."

After hearing this enlightening information, I asked Sam if she had a romantic interest of her own. She said there was someone she was very fond of—Joel. "But, you see," she said, "it's not just about that kind of energy exchange. We like to do a lot of the same stuff."[4]

In almost every session since then, Joel has been there in the background. I don't know if he comes because he's hanging around Sam at that time or if he wants to be available when there's a question about him.

Sam and Joel spend a great deal of time together. They both enjoy outdoor activities, including hiking, biking, horseback riding, and exploring. Some of the places they visit are here on earth. Sam especially enjoys visiting the Red Rocks out west. The two of them have even ridden mountain bikes around them.[5] She's mentioned exploring the Red Rocks four different times.[6]

Both Sam and Joel love playing music and singing. Though music is an important part of Sam's soul, Joel is more gifted in that area. He can pick up any instrument

---

3. JD, July 16, 2019; JD, October 29, 2019
4. JD, May 13, 2019
5. JD, May 13, 2019; JD, July 2, 2019
6. GK, January 29, 2016; JD, May 13, 2019; JD, August 15, 2019; JD, March 5, 2020

and play it. Sam usually sings while Joel plays music.[7] *Joel admitted he isn't quite the artist she is. So, they balance each other out.*[8]

They also spend time with animals. During one conversation, Sam showed them riding horses and performing stunts. And in Sam's typical fun-loving manner, she showed off. At first, they were on a dirt track jumping over equestrian gates. Then suddenly a staircase of clouds opened up, and they galloped up to another level, where there were more gates to jump over.[9]

Joel lived here while Sam was my daughter. He grew up in a rural area of the Midwest and died in an accident.[10] *"He got here after I did." Sam said he wasn't somebody she knew in this life, but he was somebody her soul already knew on the other side.*[11] *She's known him the equivalent of two hundred years, so she described him as new, but not brand new. They've had at least one life together here. And at the time of my introduction to Joel, they were not soulmates. I asked if they were in different soul families. In response, Sam made a joke. "Yes, we're in different soul families. But it's not like the Montagues and the Capulets" (from* Romeo and Juliet*).*[12]

After they'd been together a little while, Sam told me more about her activities with Joel. "We don't do everything together. That's just not how it works over here." They both have things they need to do by themselves, like lessons or projects.[13] *"We're all working on different things and growing in different ways and [doing] whatever we want to do." She says much of what they're working on individually is*

---

7. JD, July 2, 2019; JD, August 15, 2019
8. JD, July 2, 2019
9. JD, October 8, 2019
10. JD, June 15, 2019
11. JD, May 13, 2019
12. JD, July 16, 2019
13. JD, October 11, 2019

similar, though, so they do a lot together.[14]

My heart swells every time Sam shares details about her relationship with Joel. And when I think back on her longing for romantic love here, I feel immense relief. Sam admitted, "This is the kind of connection I wanted when I was there—what I would have wanted to find. But it wasn't for me to find there." And while that may have been sad when she was here, she said, "It's not sad now. It's how it was supposed to be there. I know this is hard to imagine. Really, when you get over here, none of your experiences that you had were sad. We don't look at them as being sad because we look at everything and see why it was and why we needed it."[15] Again, Sam reminded me that life as a human is more about the lessons we need to learn in order to grow spiritually.

A few months later, Sam again brought up her earthly challenges regarding finding a romantic connection. "It's easier for me over here than it was in this last lifetime." Sam admitted she really struggled with physical love here. "I had body issues. And that's all gone."[16]

Once, when I asked what the two of them had been doing, Sam showed herself floating on a raft in the water. She said they were doing a lot of relaxing and having deep conversations. She explained, "When you're having this sort of disconnection, it's good to talk about everything that you've experienced that helps you to grow. You talk about 'These are the things that I've been doing and experiencing and felt and learned.' We still need to learn like that over here. We don't know everything over here. And we haven't had every experience either." But she did confirm that there's a real difference between the experiences on the other side and the experiences on earth. They're very different.[17]

---

14. JD, November 18, 2019
15. JD, June 15, 2019
16. JD, October 11, 2019
17. JD, August 24, 2019

More on Soulmates

Exactly five months after telling me about Joel, Sam revealed the two of them officially had a soulmate connection. As mentioned before, we all have multiple soulmates. Sam explained that soulmate connections take a long time to form. This can happen when two souls bond on the other side or spend lifetimes together here. She said, "We can have soulmates that form strictly on the other side and don't come into lives with us." Because Joel and Sam enjoy each other and feel strongly bonded, they naturally became soulmates.

I asked if one of them had to leave their soul family. "The soul families are constantly growing and changing," Sam explained. "It's not like there's just fifteen people in our soul family and nobody else can ever be in it. People can come in and out of our soul families. They can go into others. They can move around." So, Joel has moved to her soul family—which is also my soul family.[18]

It occurred to me that if Sam and I are major soulmates and know each other extremely well, I must have met Joel before. When I asked Sam about this, she said Joel and I definitely know each other.[19]

Appearance in Heaven

Curious about what Joel looked like, I asked about his preferred appearance. I already knew Sam enjoyed changing up her look. At the beginning of this particular session, she had shown up with long blonde braids and wearing jeans and a T-shirt.

Since Sam prefers being a female, she usually chooses to have female attributes. She said, "Sometimes I like my boobs to be big. Sometimes I like them to be small. Sometimes I

---

18. JD, October 11, 2019
19. JD, May 4, 2020

like big hips. Sometimes I like small hips."

Not surprisingly, she said that I also prefer the female body. Sam said I like being feminine and graceful, like a tall, thin dancer. But she pointed out that I've been all kinds of shapes and sizes in different lives, just as she has.

Joel definitely prefers the male form. He doesn't change his appearance as much as Sam does. At the time of my inquiry, he looked to be in his twenties, with a lean, muscular, and masculine body. His hair was shoulder-length, and he wore a plaid shirt. Looking clean-cut, he had the feel of a metro-farmer—someone who would have a garden on a roof in the city.

Sam went on to explain, "We do have preferences for how we appear physically." For spirits that have had many lives, there are many features to choose from. Spirits don't have to choose a look from a physical life, but Sam said there's usually a collection of favorite attributes that a soul has had throughout lifetimes.[20]

More on Romance and Sex

Since Sam and I have been around for a long time, we've each had a great number of romantic connections. "It's in the hundreds," she said. "We're eternal beings. Why wouldn't it be?" Most souls, she said, have had hundreds of romantic connections. "We can have romantic relations over here with a soul we've never gone into a life with."

She said there are also plenty of humans who go into lifetimes wanting to be celibate. They don't feel the need for a physical connection. This lack of interest came with them from the other side. It's in their soul's DNA.[21]

---

20. JD, October 11, 2019
21. JD, April 13, 2020

Who Is Sam?

MESSAGES FROM SAM: During the week of the fourth anniversary of her passing, Sam divulged something new about our relationship. First, she thanked me for giving her the opportunity to come into a life that would end early. She stressed the difficulty of losing a child, and then reminded me that it was in both her contract and mine to experience her early departure. But on this day, she added the important fact that our conversations after her death had also been planned.[1]

It had never occurred to me that our communications between earth and heaven were part of our plan. However, it did confirm that I had been guided to find a way to communicate with Sam. And this exciting news explained so much. Not only had Sam been comforting me via our conversations, but she'd made it possible for me to get to know more about who she really is. I had also been given the opportunity to learn more about heaven, and in turn, I could share this information with others.

So, who is Sam? Throughout these past five years, I've come to know more of the characteristics that define the soul I call Sam. And from what the mediums have relayed, the characteristics depicted in our sessions definitely encompass my daughter's personality. I've been told that spirits come

---

1. JD, July 2, 2019

through as we knew them here. Otherwise, we wouldn't know or believe it's them.

I love to hear mediums describe Sam, especially when they first meet her. They frequently characterize her as carefree, happy-go-lucky, uplifting, sweet, kindhearted, gentle, playful, cute, funny, theatrical, passionate, analytical, smart, stubborn, patient, impatient, and sassy. To some extent, these qualities all fit the person I knew here.

From the other side, Sam gets impatient only when mediums ramble on about their personal experiences, or if they can't clearly hear her. Sometimes, she crosses her arms, taps her feet, or puts her hands on her hips to get across her frustration.

But she's always patient with me. Sassiness is the one characteristic that I didn't see displayed in her life here, as much as I would have liked. However, she's often sassy from the other side.

MESSAGES FROM SAM: Sam acknowledged that most of her personality from this life is part of who she is now. And prompted by my many questions on the subject, she explained the difference between our soul's personality and a specific personality in one of our lives.

She said our soul carries through from lifetime to lifetime. Although we have a different personality in each life, the same soul remains with us. The complete soul—or "higher self"—is the collection of all the experiences that the soul has had in every life and on the other side. As a human, our personality is independent of our soul, because so much of our soul knowledge has been blocked from us. And when we cross over, that individual personality becomes part of the higher self—the complete soul.

Sam continued, "It's not like my soul before this life was a completely different energy." Sam's interests and the lessons that she was learning in this life were based on who her soul already is. "We develop as souls in each life that we have." Even though our personalities in the human form are separate from the soul, these personalities add to the soul on the other side. She also said, "Just like no two humans are alike, no two souls on this side are alike."

Concerned that Sam will be different when I cross over, I told her that I wanted her personality to be the same as the one I knew and loved. She said it will be, and that I will definitely recognize her.[2]

Whenever I think of Sam's challenges and any unhappiness she might have experienced here, I quickly remind myself that she is home now, where she can fully express her personality and where she's surrounded by love.

Sam has a life full of adventure, creativity, fun, rewarding work, and unimaginable love. And as a mother, I'm relieved and overjoyed knowing she's living a life that surpasses any dreams that I had for her while she was here.

---

2. JD, July 16, 2019

Sam's Final Message

As I as worked on finishing our story—this book—Sam offered her hopes and dreams for me: "That you will find peace. That you will find comfort. That you will find contentment. And that you will truly know the love that I felt for you."

And when I asked Sam to share one universal message for all of us, she immediately responded, "Love and compassion." She said we need to love one another, even if we don't like one another. And we need to have compassion for each other because we don't know what others are experiencing in their lives. She added that not being judgmental or critical is a part of this.[3]

More than once Sam has told me, "It's all about love," and that after we arrive in heaven, we will ask ourselves, "What did we learn about love?"[4]

---

3. JD, September 3, 2020
4. GK, July 5, 2018; JD, September 3, 2020

Acknowledgments

Sam, if you hadn't insisted that I journal our story, this book never would have been written. And I wouldn't have had the excuse to neglect everything else these past two and a half years.

Jennifer Doran, I will forever be grateful to you for opening up Sam's world to me. Because of your beautiful spirit and amazing gift, Sam and I found the conduit we had been searching for. We both adore you.

Max, you are the epitome of a loving and supportive spouse. I know that you dreaded reading my book, fearing that you would have to give me your honest opinion. I thank God that you enjoyed it. And I thank you for your voluminous suggestions—some of which were brilliant. I'm also appreciative that you turned down sports on the TV while I wrote.

Mom, your constant support meant more than I can express, especially when everyone else thought I had gone off the deep end. Thank you for believing in me.

To my editors, I want to say thank you for sharing your talents and expertise. I wouldn't have crossed the finish line without you. Teja, it is your kindhearted reassurance that kept me going when my inexperience got the better of me. Rachel and Kimberly, your insightful perspectives led me to dig deeper and your proofreading was a godsend.

To my book designers, David and Christopher, I am in awe of your creative talents. Thank you for bringing Sam's vision to life.

About the Author

Beverly Holliday, a former teacher and artist, spends her days writing, walking, and playing with her goats. She lives with her husband, a plumber and terrific cook, in a cottage in Tallahassee, Florida. The two enjoy taking day trips to the beach, watching movies, and reading novels to each other.

As a result of her health issues, she lives an isolated life. But through communications with her daughter, she never feels alone. And she is constantly uplifted by the details of Sam's rich life in heaven. From this knowledge, she finds inspiration and motivation to write, in the hopes of bringing comfort to others.

Connect with the author by email at messagesfromsam@yahoo.com.

www.ingramcontent.com/pod-product-compliance
Lightning Source LLC
Chambersburg PA
CBHW072004110526
44592CB00012B/1197